PLANTING
DESIGN
ESSENTIALS

PLANTING DESIGN
ESSENTIALS

Jill Anderson and Pamela Johnson

THE CROWOOD PRESS

First published in 2011 by
The Crowood Press Ltd
Ramsbury, Marlborough
Wiltshire SN8 2HR

www.crowood.com

British Library Cataloguing-in-Publication Data
A catalogue record for this book is available from the British Library.

ISBN 978 1 84797 270 5

Photographs by: Pamela Johnson, Jill Anderson, Clive Nichols and Gethyn Davies.
Artwork, graphics and Photoshop by: Pamela Johnson, Jill Anderson and Gethyn Davies.

Typeset by Servis Filmsetting Ltd, Stockport, Cheshire
Printed and bound in Singapore by Craft Print International

CONTENTS

FOREWORD

Planting design is a fascinating thing, but is not for the faint hearted. I often describe it to my students as the loss leader of garden design, not in an attempt to disparage but in order to prepare them for the agony and the ecstasy to come in what is by any standards a time-consuming exercise.

You have been warned!

I am full of admiration for Jill and Pamela in their determination to sort out the planting design process and to provide the much-needed guidelines that will surely help us all to achieve better and longer lasting results. It is true that there are many limiting factors that will help us to plant appropriately – an understanding of pH, soil type, drainage, shade, exposure and so on. But, these considerations are little more than the tip of the iceberg, for the plant kingdom is immense and the variations available to us in creating successful combinations and associations are almost infinite – and this is where the head-scratching and the long list of questions begin.

Colour, whether delivered through flower, fruit, foliage or stem is a major concern along with seasonality. When is the colour to be delivered and how does this work with the rest of our selections? What about texture and the size or scale of foliage or the pattern of stems and branches? The heights and density of planting need to be structured in some way, perhaps to screen or to enclose spaces. This requires careful three-dimensional thinking. Are the plants compatible ecologically? Are they aggressive self-seeders or literally shrinking violets?

There are so many options and a flick through a favourite reference book or nursery catalogue will simply lengthen the many lists that gardeners, designers and plant fiends grow accustomed to as they plough on. Asking for advice or thoughts from others can simply prolong the agony as favourites are suggested that are probably not even on your list.

In Britain, often seen as the home of gardens and planting design, we experience a climate that is moderate and benign, allowing a huge range of species to grow relatively happily. This is coupled with a long history of plant collecting from across the globe producing a huge diversity in our gardens on the one hand, coupled with overwhelming complexity on the other. Design is about coherence and consistency, the search for unity, structure and order in some way.

So, what to do?

Well, firstly a decisive approach is essential. One could sit for days dreaming about wonderful options for our gardens and landscapes that remain just that. It is much better to have a go and make mistakes than never to plant at all. Plants are generally quite forgiving and rarely mind being re-located, especially if it is for the better.

But, perhaps more importantly we need to organize our thinking first so that we can act more efficiently later. What is the planting for? Where is it to be located? What do we want it to do? When will it look its best? How tall should the planting grow? These are just some of the questions that we can ask and answer before trailing through pages of plant listings. This preparatory rigour prevents us using species on a whim or because they suddenly beguile as they come into view in glorious technicolour in the catalogue.

The imposition of an order or a structure to the design process helps us to know what we are looking for and to go in search of it. Once furnished with our shortlist, we can then start to organize and sort the planting into groups and associations. Much has changed in this respect over the last decade or so with plant groups or masses growing in scale. With designers such as Piet Oudolf, Tom Stuart Smith and Dan Pearson using plants in tens or even hundreds, the emphasis has changed. The old plant-collecting mentality with perhaps species groups of three or five at the most is now outdated with larger groups reflecting light, providing stronger colour and more distinct textural interest. These larger groups move in the breeze, creating a more dynamic picture even in smaller scale gardens and the transparency of grasses allows a luminous quality that woody planting was never able to offer.

At last we see the planting palette simplifying but the impact of the planting increasing as the pendulum swings in favour of design – and long may it swing that way. But don't take my word for it. The following pages expand on these themes to entice and draw you in to the planting design process from the early tentative stages of planning and design thinking to the ordering, planting and subsequent maintenance of the schemes you might produce.

For all its intricacies and frustrations, planting design remains a glorious pleasure and one to which I am always drawn. Such an enthusiasm is clearly evident within this book; read on and prepare to be enthralled.

Andrew Wilson
Assessor and judge, RHS show gardens
Director, The London College of Garden Design
Author and garden designer

Part of a long border along the main terrace of a house in Surrey. The planting is designed to create a sense of movement in different forms, as a river might take on different characteristics.

INTRODUCTION

An attractive composition of shapes and colour.

Gardening appeals to so many people because it's such a great source of enjoyment. We all recognize that beautiful gardens are a pleasure to spend time in; they have a personality and atmosphere all of their own, reflecting the individuality of their owners and the character of their location. In modern times we're fortunate to have a wide range of plants at our disposal, a legacy not only of the plant hunters who

risked life and limb to bring back interesting plants from abroad, but also of the present-day plant breeders who have increased the choice, raising new plant varieties with fabulous characteristics.

However, choosing from such an enormous variety of plants can be daunting. We must take into account numerous factors such as the practical conditions in the garden: the type of soil, sun, shade and prevailing weather conditions, as well as our personal preferences of style and colour. So, how do we choose plants that will flourish? Which ones make good companions that not only grow well but will look good side by side? How can we garden in a sustainable manner and work with nature rather than against it?

CREATING A PLANTING PLAN

Perhaps you're relatively happy with most of the planting in your garden, but have a few problem areas where it's difficult to grow anything. Maybe some of the plant combinations look a bit dull and uninteresting, and you just want some new ideas. At the other end of the scale you may be at a complete loss as to where to start improving the planting and you're looking for ideas and a clear direction.

The answer to all these dilemmas is a well-considered planting plan that will generate a list of plants that are perfect for your garden and compatible with the existing plants. The process of compiling the plan is explained in simple steps in the following chapters, in such a way that once the principles are understood, the process can be applied to a variety of situations. The aim is to avoid the frustration that many gardeners face because they just can't get their garden to look right. A simple sketched plan of the garden will help you to focus your ideas about what changes to make, allowing you to try out different ideas and make endless adjustments until you are confident with the final plan.

Displays of plants in garden centres can be very attractive, and we are all tempted to make a spontaneous purchase; back home we wander round the garden trying to decide where to put the plant. The final decision is usually based on available space rather than a position that will really suit the plant. As a result the plant may or may not survive; it may ultimately grow too big or turn out to be the wrong colour. This approach to planting inevitably builds up an eclectic collection of plants randomly bought over time, giving the garden a disjointed appearance.

Of course, some experimentation with plants is part of the fun of gardening. Garden designers often try out new plants in their own garden to see how they

A perfect combination of variety, colour and texture.

develop, so that they can use them with confidence in a client's garden. Most gardeners love buying and acquiring new plants, but whilst there's no doubt that an interesting and inexpensive plant will be worth buying, for the overall success of your garden it would be better to stick to your planned planting list and avoid disappointment later. If the temptation cannot be resisted, then at least find out some details about a new plant before you buy, to establish that it will be suitable in your garden setting. You may have a small, urban garden where a smart, formal planting

scheme will be just right; or a sprawling rural garden where there's plenty of room for a colourful, riotous, selection of plants. Devising your own planting plan will help you to find plants that will suit both you and your garden.

The whole process using this approach is enjoyable because everything will be under your control, and the garden will ultimately have a combination of plants that will give you great pleasure. Moreover it will undoubtedly save you money in the long run because you will only buy plants that are suitable for your garden. The implementation of the plan can be done at your own pace and could be carried out in convenient stages if there is a lot to do. The goal to aim for is a garden that not only looks beautiful, but is also practical to use and flows together forming a complete and beautiful picture.

DESIGNING YOUR GARDEN

Planting design can be described as a pleasing composition of plants where the shapes, colours and textures combine together to enhance each other, and are appropriate for the conditions and landscape where they will be planted. The design is most successful when all the attributes of shape, colour, seasonality and structure are woven together to create a pleasing whole, and the garden becomes more than the sum of its parts.

However, for real success in the long term, it is also important to have an understanding of how plants grow, and why they prefer to grow in certain conditions. Both the aesthetics of design and the practical issues of horticulture will be discussed throughout the book.

Cool restful planting.

There are any number of factors to understand and take into account when creating a planting plan, for example:

- Compatibility of plants with your soil
- Aspect – is the planting area in sun or shade?
- Personal taste – what plants do you like, and equally importantly, what don't you like?
- Surrounding landscape – how will your plants fit in with this? (this is especially important when planting trees)
- Style of your house
- Use of the garden (no delicate plants next to where the children play football)
- Climatic conditions (vary enormously around the country, or near the coast rather than inland)
- Colour – do you want an abundance of colour in each season?
- Shapes of plants – which ones work together to provide contrast and interest?
- Seasonality – what looks good at different times of the year? Can you have interest for all the year?

Designing and putting together a planting plan is just the beginning. Plants can grow and develop in unexpected ways that may not have been part of the original plan. A planting scheme is a constant process that has to be monitored and tweaked as time goes on. Rather than being a chore, there's a great joy in having your own unique space; it's what makes gardening interesting. Continual monitoring through the seasons will help you to get to know your garden in a way that no one else will. The best results will come from giving your plants attention little and often, especially during periods of fast growth in the spring and early summer. It will help if you have the practical knowledge and skills necessary to develop the design as it matures, so that your initial vision can be realized.

Basic information outlined in the following pages will help you to manage your garden, such as:

- The ultimate size of plants
- Their rate of growth in different conditions and how to look after them
- What pruning may be needed to keep them in shape, healthy and fully productive
- How to recognize basic pests and diseases, preferably before they take hold and do too much damage to the plant.

WHY WE HAVE GARDENS

People have needed to have gardens throughout recorded history, initially simply as a place to fulfil our most basic need to grow food and provide shelter. There is evidence that the first gardens were made in Egypt in 1400BC, and we know that the Chinese, the Greeks and the Romans all placed great importance on gardens. Plants such as rue, sage and laurel were

Classic pink roses.

Vegetables growing in a raised bed.

grown in the medicinal monastery gardens during the medieval period providing herbal remedies as a basic form of medicine. Woad and chamomile were also grown and used for dying wool and fabric, as well as 'strew plants' that were grown to be placed on the floor to improve the air. Our ancestors soon realized that as well as being practical, gardens could also be places for pleasure, peace and contemplation, somewhere to express our creativity and our instinct to nurture.

Over the years gardening has changed and developed along with our social needs. In more recent times, during the Second World War, gardens became practical places as the 'Grow for Victory' campaign became a real necessity for people to provide food for their families. In the years following the war, food became cheaper, and gardens gradually became less important as places for growing food and developed more into spaces for leisure time. New introductions, such as disease-resistant rose varieties, also encouraged gardeners to become more interested in growing ornamental plants, and neat lawns and rose beds became more fashionable.

INCREASED INTEREST IN GARDENS

Although it may not feel like it, today we have more leisure time to spend on our hobbies compared to previous generations, and a number of factors have combined to make gardening and gardens even more significant today. Many people enjoy visiting gardens in their leisure time and there are certainly lots to choose from, either at the grander end of the spectrum, such as National Trust properties, Royal Horticultural Society gardens and RHS flower shows, or some of the more modest gardens that open under the National Garden Scheme. These opportunities create an awareness of different plant compositions and varieties that we may not be familiar with or, equally importantly, plant combinations that we personally don't like.

The rapid rise in the number of garden centres and the development of selling plants in plastic pots revolutionized their availability, as it became possible to buy and plant throughout the year (although in practical terms this is not advisable). There is a wide range of plants available, with new varieties being introduced every year and different types of plants becoming obtainable from abroad. Gardening programmes on television, a large assortment of gardening magazines, websites and blogs provide seasonal tips and information about what plants to grow and how to maintain them. Our interest in gardens and plants is further encouraged by having all the information we need at the touch of a button.

The growing realization that our local environment plays an important role in our mood and general well-being has further increased our interest in gardening. Given the fast pace of life, many of us use our gardens as tranquil places to escape to, or simply as private green spaces to spend our free time in. Gardening gives us the opportunity for fresh air and exercise; just pottering around is generally therapeutic and is particularly beneficial for people with chronic illnesses or mental health problems. Doctors have even reported that patients in hospital wards overlooking trees and green spaces require fewer painkillers.

Gardening gives us the chance to reduce waste and carbon emissions by adopting simple gardening techniques such as making our own compost, using water wisely and selecting appropriate plants that will grow to their full potential without using too many resources. As well as nourishing the garden soil for free, producing home compost for one year can save global warming gasses equivalent to all the CO_2 the kettle produces annually and will also divert unnecessary waste away from landfill.

A meadow of silver birches trees enclosed by yew hedges.

WHY GARDEN DESIGN IS IMPORTANT

Gardens are multi-functional and can be adapted to suit our differing needs. They provide an outdoor space to grow ornamental plants, herbs, fruit and vegetables; a safe and stimulating place for children to play and explore; and somewhere to entertain our friends and family. The garden can also be a financial asset; although that's not what motivates most of us to garden, it's nice to know that all the time and money invested can also add value to your house if the work is done well.

The garden is thought of as an outdoor room as people spend more of their leisure time outside; it's probably larger than any room in the house, so it makes sense to maximize its potential as effectively as possible. The wide range of garden accessories such as outdoor-ovens and fire-pits provide heat and enable us to eat outside instead of having to retreat inside as the evening chill sets in. Outdoor lighting, in its many forms, gives us the opportunity to be outside in the evening or to enjoy the garden from the inside on long winter evenings.

There is increasing interest in interior design and design generally, which is reflected in a desire to spend time and money furnishing and decorating our homes to reflect our personality, or simply to make life more comfortable. These changes in our lifestyles raise expectations of the possibilities of how all our surroundings could look, and this inevitably includes our gardens.

This book has been written to demystify planting design. Each chapter takes you through the whole process in a simple, logical sequence. We explain how to confidently select the right plants for your garden using criteria that are appropriate to you and the site. We describe the basic principles of garden design and the correct techniques for planting, and finally, how to look after your plants to ensure the garden matures beautifully.

Jill Anderson
www.andersonlandscapedesign.co.uk
Pamela Johnson
www.pamelajohnson.co.uk

Warm colours are energizing and uplifting.

THE PLANNING STAGE

Making a scale plan, analyzing the existing garden, writing your brief, legal constraints, basic principles of garden design

Gardens are important places for most of us, providing a green space in which to unwind at the end of a busy day, or a relaxed place for children to play and explore. Whatever type of outdoor space you have, it makes sense to enjoy it to its fullest potential.

The plants are an important element of any garden, and they can also be the most challenging. They are after all living things that don't always perform as we would like them to. Combining plants successfully requires knowledge about how they grow and the situations that they prefer. The initial approach to any changes will depend on how well you know the garden. It takes time to get to know a garden; they are dynamic spaces developing through the seasons, looking different throughout the year and sometimes even changing on a daily basis.

PLANNING A NEW GARDEN

If you have taken on a new garden, resist the temptation to make changes until you've spent time getting to know it – find out what the soil is like, where the areas are that are exposed to cold wind. It's also important to know where the sunniest spot is to sit on a spring morning, how the light changes through the seasons and where's the best place to plant those ornamental grasses so that they'll glow when back-lit by the evening sun.

Winter is the ideal time to make plans about what could be planted or to change the basic structure of the garden. There may be some choice herbaceous

OPPOSITE PAGE: **Dawn light on *Papaver orientalis* 'Beauty of Livermere'.**

Red poppies and ornamental grasses.

plants and spring bulbs already established, waiting to emerge the following year, so any digging should be done carefully. Wait until late winter, when dormant plants are beginning to appear, then you can see exactly where things are and begin to identify exactly what plants are in the garden. Spring and summer can be spent tidying-up the garden, removing weeds – especially the tough perennials such as nettles and bind-weed. They will need several attempts to remove them entirely, but they should always be removed before any new plants are put in. They will compete

Early blooms of Iris *reticulata* signal the start of spring.

with surrounding plants for water and nutrients, and because they're well established, they are more likely to be successful. Spring is a good time of year to improve the soil too and prepare it for planting (*see* Chapter 8). It can be frustrating if you are keen to make progress, so indulge your need for new plants during this period by planting up seasonal plants in attractive containers.

CHANGING A FAMILIAR GARDEN

If you have had your garden for a while you have the advantage of knowing the conditions in it, what type of soil there is and how it responds to the changing seasons. But sometimes dissatisfaction can gradually creep in, there may be problem areas where plants won't grow. Maybe the garden doesn't look how you hoped it would, and combining plants together hasn't been altogether successful.

Whilst the information here is mostly for gardeners planning their own planting, it applies just as much to garden designers planning a garden in a professional capacity, or friends who have gardening experience offering to lend a helping hand to someone with less experience. A designer will use their skills to interpret the owner's wishes, so time spent talking to the owner, finding out their likes, dislikes, general taste and preferred style is crucial. A lot of information can be obtained by observing the owner's surroundings and establishing what their personal taste is, as well as discussing the project with them. It's useful to note what type of pictures are on their walls, the choice of books on the shelves and the colours used to decorate the house – all are valuable clues. It will take a concerted effort to get to know their garden too, analyzing it as a whole, identifying existing plants and putting all the information together, then talking to the owners so that the plans and ideas are clearly communicated between all parties involved.

Advantages of Having a Scale Plan of the Garden

- You can save time and money by making changes on paper first
- View the garden as a complete picture: does it all link up?
- Make copies of the plan to show different examples of planting
- Keep a record for future use and note changes on it
- Have all the notes on one document: plants, soil type, shade, sun, etc.
- If you want to divide the garden proportionally it is easier if you have a plan
- Show areas to be screened or views from the house that could be framed

MAKING A SCALE PLAN

The first real step is to make a plan of the garden exactly as it is at the moment. When you go on to creating a planting plan, however big or small the area you wish to change, it will be so much easier if you have a simple sketch plan that is drawn to scale. Even if the changes are quite minor, a plan will give you the opportunity to see the whole garden in one go and work out if there's enough room for all the plants you'd like, and you'll see how any changes will work within the existing framework.

If the house is new or has been extended, you may be able to obtain existing plans from an architect or developer. They may not be accurate if they've been enlarged or reduced, so check their accuracy by comparing measurements of the plan with one or two features in the garden. (If the garden is very large it may be easier to commission a professional surveyor to plot the garden accurately.)

How to Make a Scale Plan

You can scale down the measurements onto graph paper so that everything in the garden fits conveniently onto one piece of paper. (A4 graph paper is available from stationers, but you'll probably need a larger sized sheet of paper, which can be bought from art shops.)

At a 1:50 scale, 2cm (approx. 1in) represents 1 metre (39in) so a 10-metre (approx. 33ft) length of fencing will measure 20cm (8in) on the paper, which is useful for the average garden. If you have a larger garden you could use a scale of 1:100, then 20 metres would measure 20cm.

You'll need two tape measures, 30m and a 5m. First you measure the outline of the house, and the boundaries in relation to the house and gradually add all the other dimensions of the garden.

Where to Start

Start by measuring the house walls adjacent to the part of the garden you're going to be planning. Draw them onto a sheet of graph paper to the scale you have chosen.

Note where the sun rises: if it's behind you as you stand in the garden, then north point is on your right. Mark this on your plan so that you can work out where the sunny and shady areas of your garden are during the day. This will be one of the relevant facts when choosing plants.

How to Position Main Features on the Plan

The main features are added using triangulation, which is simply a method of accurately indicating the location of features such as an isolated tree in the middle of a lawn, which would otherwise be difficult to position accurately on a plan. This third point, the tree, is located using its relationship to two known points, such as the corners of the house. As well as graph paper, a pair of compasses and scale ruler are needed for this.

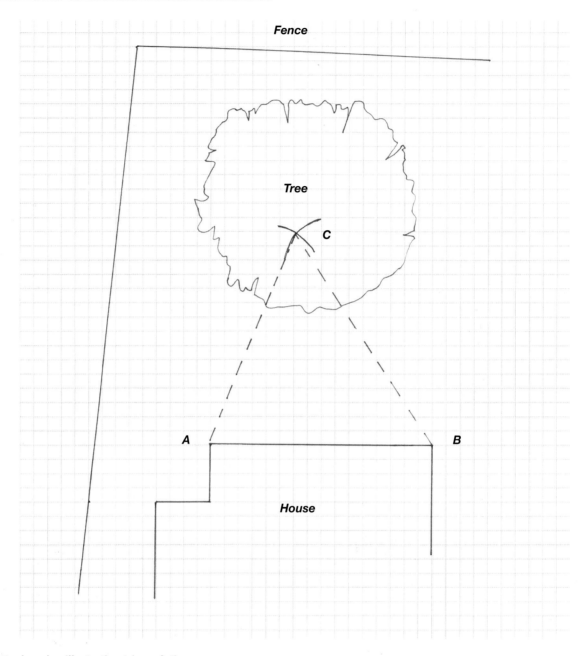

Garden plan illustrating triangulation.

First draw a base-line between two permanent features, such as the wall of the house: A is one corner, B is the other. Note the measurement from A to the tree (C). Note the measurement from B to the tree (C).

Using the ruler draw the baseline (A–B) to scale on the graph paper. Extend the compass and measure the length A–C on the scale ruler. Position the spike of the compass on A and draw an arc.

Repeat the process for B–C, placing the compass spike on B, and draw an arc to cross the first arc. Where the two arcs cross each other will be point C, indicating the position of the tree.

This method can be used to determine the position of other elements of the garden, such as the corners of the boundaries.

initial notes that you made earlier about the plants, trees and large plants can now be accurately marked on the plan.

ANALYZING THE EXISTING GARDEN

Try to identify exactly what plants are already growing there; if the precise names aren't known, make a note of the size and whether they are evergreen or deciduous.

Next have an objective look at the plants that thrive and those that struggle. Which ones have never looked quite right where they are – maybe they're too big, or the wrong shape or colour? Make a note of all your initial thoughts about these plants, including ones that you definitely want to keep and others you may be considering removing.

Use the plan to note down the conditions in the garden, such as cold winds, the sunny and shady areas or low-lying areas of clay soil that can be soggy for much of the year. There may be views of neighbouring buildings to be screened from your garden or a lovely view to be framed by a gap in the planting. The

WRITING YOUR BRIEF

Professional designers have developed a process to make decisions about each gardening project. They begin by gathering information to determine the choices of plants that will suit you and your garden; it's a thought process that generates a list of ideas. It will clarify all the constraints and possibilities that need to be taken into account and encourage you to think about the opportunities for the garden. The finished result is more likely to be successful because it's been well thought through.

Gathering Information

By visiting gardens and horticultural shows, you can learn more about plants and how they combine together. Take a notebook and camera with you to record what you see. Build up a record of the type of

Good design can be used to change a problem area (left) into an asset (right); here a pond has been created in a low-lying area of soggy clay soil.

Visit flower shows for ideas and inspiration.

plants that you like, what colour combinations catch your eye and which contrasting shapes appeal to you. Cut out pictures of plants and gardens that you like from magazines and newspapers. Inspiration doesn't just have to come from obvious sources; you may also be inspired by sculpture, buildings or soft furnishings. Include pictures of all of these and examples of favourite colours or experiment with combinations of ones that you don't normally use.

You may be a gardening novice with relatively little knowledge or experience, or a more experienced gardener who hasn't used this orderly approach before. Ideas take time to evolve, so be patient and gather as much relevant information as possible and learn to trust your judgement. Make sure that your garden will reflect your character and personality, because that's what will make it unique.

Matching Your Garden to Your Life Style

Above all, the garden must suit you and your family's life style. How much free time have you got? One of the most important factors to consider at this stage is how much time you can spend maintaining the garden. Some plants need more maintenance than others; for example, herbaceous plants need regular dead-heading to keep them flowering and then require dividing every three years, whilst most evergreen shrubs need little regular maintenance. A garden filled only with shrubs and low-maintenance plants changes little through the seasons, and can look static and dull. The ratio between low-maintenance shrubs and high-maintenance plants will depend mainly on the amount of time you have to look after them. Choosing the right plants can make the

A new border two years after planting.

difference between your garden being happily within your control or unmanageable. Depending on the size of the garden and the time that you have, a combination of different types of plants is a safe bet, allowing variety and interest through the year. But if you are short of time, planting an area with just one species of plant is a technique that works well in a contemporary setting; blocks of tall ornamental grasses can look very effective used this way.

How long do you plan to live in the house? This may determine how much time and money you want to spend on the garden. If you see your garden as temporary, herbaceous plants may be the best option because they are usually cheaper and grow more quickly than most shrubs.

What plants have you already got? Consider which existing large plants are worth keeping – it's a more sustainable way of gardening, and their mature size will contribute height and volume to a border. Neglected but healthy plants can be renovated or creatively pruned to give them a new lease of life.

Looking at photos of your garden will reveal things that you may not have noticed. It's a good method of focusing on particular areas without being distracted by the larger scene. This technique may also help you become more aware of parts of the garden that are uninteresting. Look at photos of the garden from different times of the year, so that the planting can be planned to provide something of interest to see all year round. Pay particular attention to the part of the garden that is seen from the house in winter, where you should avoid using only deciduous plants.

If you're new to the area, have a look and see what type of plants are growing and doing well in neighbouring gardens; they may not be exactly what you want in your garden, but they will provide clues about the soil type.

A lovely balance of flowers and shrubs.

Gathering Information

The plan needs to take into account the different requirements of all the people using it.

Will there be enough lawn for children to play on? Does the grass need to be tough enough to withstand children's games? Consider those who visit the garden on a regular basis, such as elderly people and young children; appropriate planting or structural planting may need to be incorporated to make the garden safe. What are the requirements of anyone with disabilities who uses the garden? Paths need to be wider than usual to accommodate wheelchair users. What facilities or equipment do you need to include, such as a shed, bicycle or toy storage, clothes drying, paths for access? What type of planting will be needed near these areas?

What is the overall vision for the garden?

Think hard about how you want the whole garden to look and develop. What do you like and dislike about it? Would you like more colourful flowers, or plants with more perfume? Would you like some climbing plants on the house? How will the planting be affected if the shape of the garden needs changing? Do you want plants at the boundaries, such as hedges rather than fences? Have you considered the future use of the garden? Can changes be easily incorporated?

What are your limitations?

How much time can be spent looking after the garden to keep it maintained? Do you have the time and skills for plants that require regular pruning? How much will it all cost?

Try not to rush into any decisions before a plan has been completed and all possibilities have been considered. It's worth spending time on this part of the procedure, because the final results will stem from this initial process. This disciplined approach does work – it's the tried and tested process that professional garden designers use for their clients. If you need help with this process, then you may want to engage a professional garden designer for some advice. Once you have gone through the process of gathering information as described here you will have a clearer idea of what you want and be more able to communicate your ideas.

Your Conclusions

This is the time to write down your conclusions, making a list of all the elements you want to include in your new plan. Collect all the photos, magazine pages and colour swatches and stick them on a large piece of paper. These two items – the plan and the inspiration ideas – will be the basis on which you make your choices about the style of the garden and the type of plants you want.

The following examples may relate to you, but if not they will give you some ideas of what to include on the list.

Growing Family

(Short on time but with lots of different requirements for their garden)

- A safe but interesting place for the children to play
- Tough plants to withstand children playing and kicking a ball near them
- Plant screening for storage of toys and tools
- A lawn
- Somewhere to grow vegetables and soft fruit, with a compost heap and water butts
- Scented plants to surround the terrace
- They may be away in school holidays, so want plants of interest at other times of the year
- Interesting, attractive low-maintenance plants

Young Single Professional Person

(First house or flat with a small garden)

- Low-maintenance plants
- Garden is mostly shady, so needs appropriate plants
- No lawn
- A place to entertain friends: needs a paved area for table and chairs to entertain friends, would like scented planting nearby
- A pergola to enclose a patio, provide shade in summer and screening from neighbours
- Specific planting, i.e. strong architectural shapes
- Likes trees

Retired Couple

(Perhaps have a large garden and enjoy gardening as a hobby)

- The garden has poor soil, so appropriate plants are required
- Somewhere sheltered to sit so that they can enjoy the garden all year round
- Some structural planting to divide the garden and encourage a route round the garden
- Vegetable beds (including herbs), a greenhouse, cold-frames, compost heaps, water-butts

- A lawn
- Borders for shrubs and flowers for cutting
- Structures that need climbing plants
- Enjoy maintenance and like propagating their own plants and growing them for others
- Fruit trees

Busy Young Couple Living in an Urban Area

- Terrace for entertaining where scented plants would be welcome
- Bike storage that will need plant screening
- No lawn
- Low-maintenance plants
- Lush planting with some seasonal interest
- They enjoy cooking so would like herbs in the garden
- Screening of neighbour's house

LEGAL CONSTRAINTS

Apart from your own personal constraints, such as time and budget, there could be legal limitations that may have to be taken into account before any work begins. It's important to be aware of these issues at the planning stage, otherwise you may waste time thinking about incorporating features that may not be possible or will require planning permission. If you carry out work without the necessary permission there is a risk of being fined and being required to reinstate. Listed below are some of the limitations that may apply to your garden, but you are strongly advised to check all these issues with your local authority for advice and a clear idea of what is possible before starting any work.

Sites of special scientific interest and conservation areas – whose character has been designated as worth preserving because it is of special scientific, architectural or historic interest – are all subject to restrictions. A quick phone call to your local council will establish if your garden is affected by these restrictions and what you will be allowed to do.

A boundary fence softened by trees.

Tree preservation orders are made by local authorities to protect particular trees, even if they are on private land. If your trees are protected by these restrictions, you will need permission from the local tree officer (contact your local council to speak to them) before you begin any work, such as thinning branches or felling. There are substantial fines for any work being carried out without permission.

It's not always clear who owns the walls and fences that form the garden boundaries. There are no general rules about who owns what, so it's a good idea to be clear about this in case you want to change them. You may need to check the title deeds to your property or ask a solicitor to do so. You will need permission if you want to attach anything to a neighbour's boundary wall or fence.

If possible find out where the services (water, sewage pipes and cables) are so that these can be avoided when you're digging below ground. It will be useful to make a note of them on your plan if you do establish what's underground. There are regulations now about placing cables and pipes deep under ground and covering them with brightly coloured plastic warning tape, but this wasn't always the case,

and cables that were positioned years ago are often just under the surface and may not be made from armoured cabling, so take care.

Since October 2008, planning permission is necessary if more than five square metres of impermeable paving is being used in a front garden. This is to deal with the problem of flooding, due in part to a large number of front gardens being paved over and rainwater being diverted onto roads and pavements instead of being absorbed into the earth.

BASIC PRINCIPLES OF GARDEN DESIGN

As well as the functional aspects of the garden, and the legal and practical constraints, it's important to think next about the aesthetics of the garden. The most effective method is to apply the basic principles of garden design. These simple guidelines will provide an overview of the whole garden. Understanding and using them will help you to decide what type of plants to use and where to place them.

Balance

Balance is nearly always present in a symmetrical design. Placing clipped shrubs of equal size at either side of an entrance is a simple example. However, balance can also be achieved by using a combination of different size plants, such as planting a large shrub on one side balanced by three smaller ones, to create similar volume on the other side.

Harmony

Harmony is achieved by the symmetry of a number of elements in the garden working together to achieve a whole composition. It's closely related to balance, proportion and scale.

Proportion

Proportion can be interpreted as the relevant size of elements in relation to each other. The dimensions of the house, the garden – and to some extent their surroundings – should all be in proportion. If hedges on three sides of a garden are too tall for the relative space

Large rhododendrons are perfectly in scale in spacious woodlands.

they surround, they will look domineering. Marking out and adjusting the sizes of the main components on a paper plan will give you a good idea of what the proportions should be. You can also mark them out on the ground with canes and rope and view them from different angles of the house and garden, including an upstairs window, to see what works.

Volume and Scale

Unlike planning a room in a house, even small gardens are spacious, and the scale is very different because of the expanse of sky and the size of the surroundings, whether they are buildings or large trees. Items in a garden can become dwarfed and lost when set against a rural backdrop or a large building; conversely plants that are too large for the space can dominate it.

Unity

Unity is a sense of rhythm that's created in a space by repeating an element in different parts of the garden. It could be achieved by using the same type of plant or a particular colour and repeating it through the garden. It's another method of pulling all the elements together to create harmony.

Focal Points

Focal points are features in the garden for the eye to focus on. A scene without a focal point can either be dull and lacking interest or it might appear too busy without an obvious point that the eye is drawn to. Where focal points are plants, they are often referred to as a specimen plants; they usually have a strong shape different from their surroundings and are as much a piece of decoration as sculpture and artwork would be. It could be a topiary shape or a small elegant tree, such as a Japanese maple, if the conditions allow. Shrubs in containers raised on a small plinth will have more impact as a focal point, but they will need watering. A focal point can also be made by

A classic focal point at Loseley House.

A big, red frilly poppy brightens a summer day.

creating a porthole in a hedge, but there has to be something worth looking at through the hole. Views can be framed by clever use of hedging and structural shrubs such as topiary.

Simplicity

The lack of simplicity in a design results in a garden that's too fussy and won't be a comfortable place to relax in. It can happen when we try to include bit of everything, with the result that there are too many different colours and shapes competing for attention. Notice how successful planting designs in magazines, or in gardens that we visit, use fewer species in large numbers. Be prepared to edit, and remember that 'less is more'.

Try to consider all these principles of design at the planning stage, build them into the plan – and stick to it.

ASSESSING AND DEVELOPING YOUR PLAN

Putting Plants into Perspective

Plants work hard through the seasons providing colour, shape, height, texture and scent and can be a relatively inexpensive component of a garden. They are probably the most visible part of a garden and can have a lot of impact. Given the availability and relative low cost of many plants, it's easy to rely on them as the main element of the garden.

However, for the planting to be successful, in the early stages of planning think of plants as just one element in the garden. They are one component of the three-dimensional framework that is made up of boundaries and buildings such as sheds and sum-merhouses. The most successful gardens, however informal, have their planting within a strong frame-work.

Making Changes to Your Plan

Using the plan of your garden, the brief and the principles of garden design, turn your attention to developing the changes you wish to make to the garden.

Make copies of the plan and sketch out different planting ideas to see how they look. Consider the existing overall layout and shape of the garden, the position of the paths, patio, shed and how big the lawn and borders are in relation to each other. In small gardens it's tempting to make the lawn too large in an attempt to make the garden seem bigger, leaving too little space for surrounding borders. There should be a balanced ratio between the areas of hard landscape (paths and patios) and the planted areas of shrub borders and lawns. Try to avoid simply using leftover space for planting the borders – these should be a positive element of the design.

If you decide to change the structure, take note that conditions in the garden will change. If the shed is re-positioned or a new pergola built, shade will be created that wasn't there before, altering the light levels and different plants that thrive in low light will be needed.

If only one part of the garden is being changed, make sure that it fits in well with the rest of the garden in a unified way.

Thinking Three-dimensionally

It may be difficult at first to work out what the three-dimensional garden will look like in a two-dimensional plan form, but using photos of the garden from different angles will help to make things clearer. Look at the garden from an upstairs window if possible to see how the plan looks in relation to the existing garden, but use this information as a guide only, because sometimes the eye can be fooled. Take some photos from this view to help with the planning stage and keep a record of the changes that will be made.

You have taken the initial crucial steps and you now have a plan of your existing garden, with a clear idea of the changes that you want to make and how the garden could look in the future. The following chapters will give you information about appropriate plants, the style of your garden and how to plan the planting. As the ideas take shape you'll have a realistic idea of the scope of the work to be done, and can start planning how the work is going to be carried out and how much it will cost, the best time of year to carry it out (*see* Chapter 8), and whether you will need some professional assistance to prepare the garden or help with the planting.

Pleached trees define an area of planting.

WHERE DOES YOUR GARDEN GROW?

Analyzing your local area, knowing your soil, evaluating the light, assessing moisture levels, providing shelter from exposure

A winter garden under a protective layer of snow.

Is your climate warm, cold, wet or dry? What kind of soil does your garden have? Which plants grow well in the local area? All these questions need answers before you can begin to choose the right plants for your garden.

Plants grow all over the world and have adapted over millions of years to grow in their native conditions. Even if we only used plants which are native to the garden's local geography, we'd still have to

OPPOSITE PAGE: **Bright blue skies of the Mediterranean with common broom *Cytisus scoparius*.**

understand its unique conditions before knowing whether a plant will happily grow there or not. So when putting together a planting scheme with plants which may well come from another continent it is vital to understand their growing preferences and whether they are suitable for the garden you wish to grow them in.

All garden soil can be improved, but you cannot change its basic character. If the base rock beneath the soil is chalk you can't grow acid-loving plants other than in containers with ericaceous soil. If the ground is sandy and free draining those plants which like damp conditions will struggle unless there is a source of water nearby. Soil can vary from town to town and even from one street to another, and the climate can change depending on which side of the hill you live. Being familiar with and understanding the local climate, geology and growing conditions is vital when choosing plants for a garden, as is knowledge of where a plant originally came from and the conditions it has adapted to.

ANALYZING YOUR LOCAL AREA

Climate and Weather Conditions

If you have been gardening in a particular area for many years you will be more familiar with the local climate than if you've just moved from another part of the country. If you are new to an area you can find out how it's affected by the seasonal weather by enquiring at local garden centres, plant nurseries or gardening groups. Allotment holders are also a great source of valuable information, and all gardeners enjoy talking about the weather. Looking at plants growing locally will give many clues as to what the climate is like.

A city microclimate can be a few degrees warmer.

If plants such as hibiscus and tender palm trees are thriving, then the winters are probably mild and dry. Some gardeners however are unlucky and live in a frost pocket; this happens when cold air gets trapped in a dip and the land doesn't warm up as quickly as the surrounding area, and as a result plants which are unharmed elsewhere may be frosted and damaged in a frost pocket. Cities and large towns can be a few degrees warmer than the surrounding countryside due to the heat generated by the buildings and retained by bricks and concrete, resulting in a microclimate that can significantly affect the types of plants that will grow. However, a roof garden in a city can be affected by strong wind that will damage the plants and dry them out.

Geography

Hilltop gardens will be windier, colder and dryer than further down the hill, whereas at the bottom a garden will be more sheltered and the soil will probably be damp, giving quite different growing conditions. There may also be less topsoil on higher ground, as over the years it will wash down to the valley floor where it can be plentiful. Flat open

Extreme climate in Southern France with cold winters and hot summers.

Flat open country can be windswept, with coastal regions also having salt-laden air.

country will usually be wind swept; a good indication can be trees that have grown bent over due to being pushed by the wind. You often see this on the coast where constant winds shape the trees and hedges. Coastal gardens will also have salt-laden wind, which can damage plants that are not adapted to this environment.

Local Flora

Hundreds of years ago many areas of the UK were covered in forests and woodland, and in some areas we still enjoy the legacy of this in spring when the bluebell woods are in full bloom. Even in city gardens the native bluebells still persist, which indicates how well adapted they are to our soil and climate. Simply by watching which native plants, sometimes called weeds, choose to grow in our gardens tells us a great deal about the legacy left in the ground and the type of conditions we've inherited. Ground elder, nettles and comfrey all tell us that that the soil is rich and moisture retentive, whereas a self-seeded verbascum

indicates dryer poorer conditions. If you have an area in your garden where nothing will grow except the weeds, they are giving you a clue as to what the conditions are and which cultivated plants will also be happy there.

A British bluebell wood in spring.

KNOWING YOUR SOIL

Understanding soil is fundamental to understanding how plants grow. Getting to know the soil in your garden is an essential starting point, as many problems with plants can be traced back to the earth they are growing in. Soil is not a static, dead material; it is dynamic and alive and can vary from one part of the country to the next or even from street to street, garden to garden. It will change according to the seasons and the weather and is vulnerable to pollution and physical damage (*see* also Chapters 8 and 9).

Geology and Ancient History

For most of us the geology under our feet is not something we generally consider in great detail, but the soil we stand on is just the top layer of a complex geological profile made up of base rock, subsoil and topsoil. Topsoil is the layer we refer to when talking about gardens. It is the layer we dig in, plant in and work with. Beneath the topsoil is a layer called subsoil, which may be encountered when digging deep holes for planting large specimens or during construction work. Other than tree and large shrub roots very little grows in subsoil, as there is no air or food. Care must

Layers of topsoil, subsoil and base rock.

The Jurassic coastline at Kilve Beach in Somerset has visible evidence of how base rock was formed.

be taken not to contaminate topsoil with subsoil – preferably leave it undisturbed if possible.

Under the subsoil layer is the parent rock; this will determine the type of soil in your garden. Sandstone will produce sandy soil; chalk will produce chalky soil and so on. This happens in combination with the ancient geological history of a region such as forests, rivers, glaciers, plate tectonics and changing coastlines. Knowing just a little geology and ancient history of your region can help you understand a great deal about the very valuable layer of topsoil in your garden.

What is Soil?

Soil is a mixture of minute particles of rock and partially decomposed plants and animals called humus. The types of rock the soil is composed of will define it as being clay, chalk, silt, sandy or peaty. However, healthy soil will also have air, water, food and a microcosm of organisms including plants and animals. These organisms play a vital role in maintaining a healthy soil, which is the key to growing healthy

plants. The basic mineral particles in soil are usually clay, silt and sand (clay particles are the smallest and sand the largest). Your soil properties are dependant on the combination of these three different minerals.

Acidity and Alkalinity (pH Levels)

The acidity or alkalinity of your soil is dependant on the presence or absence of calcium, which is washed out of the soil by rain. If the base rock is alkaline, such as chalk or limestone, then this will leach back into the soil, which will therefore always be alkaline.

If you try to grow acid-loving plants in an alkaline soil they will at best look sickly with yellowing leaves for a while and then ultimately die. These acid-loving plants, having adapted to alkaline-free soil, are called ericaceous. Equally there are many plants – especially vegetables – which require calcium to thrive, and it is easier to increase the calcium content of soil (by adding lime) than it is to remove the calcium. Acidic soil can have lime added to it regularly when required, but alkaline soil cannot be made acidic.

Different Types of Soil

Clay soil

Because clay particles are very small, there is not much space between them for air and water. It therefore appears heavy and difficult to dig. If you take a small piece of soil and roll it between your fingers, it will easily form into a smooth ball, confirming that it is clay. A poorly draining clay soil will take longer to warm up in the spring, and the surface can crack badly in a hot dry summer. But if the particles can be separated and mixed with compost its fertility can be unlocked and it can make excellent garden soil which many plants love.

Silt

Silt is often found near rivers or reclaimed coastal land and is made up of fine particles which have been washed down from the surrounding hills over time. It is easy to dig, and the topsoil layer may be very deep. It is good for growing vegetables, being deep, fertile and moisture retentive, but can compact easily, making it difficult for lawns.

Sand

Sandy soil is also easy to dig, very free draining and warms up quickly in spring, but nutrients tend to be washed away and it can be very dry. It won't form a ball when you rub it between your fingers, but will feel gritty instead. Many plants are adapted to this type of soil, such as herbs, alpines and drought-tolerant plants.

Chalk

Chalk is a difficult soil to garden on as the topsoil is usually shallow, stony and lacking nutrients. It is also very alkaline, but again many plants have adapted to these conditions.

Peaty soil

Peaty soil is easy to work and holds water very well but can be low in nutrients and is acidic. It can make excellent garden soil when improved and can support a wide range of acid loving plants including heathers and rhododendrons.

Loam

This is what soil is expected to look like. It has a mixture of sand and clay particles, drains slowly and also retains moisture at the right levels for plants to use.

Even replacing all the topsoil will not work, as the calcium will be coming from the base rock, so it is much better to work with what you have and grow acid-loving plants in containers with ericaceous compost. Tap water often contains calcium, which can significantly affect acid-loving plants, so collected rain should be used to water plants such as rhododendrons and azaleas.

So how do you know what type of soil you have? A lot can be learned from simple observation – for instance, what plants grow nearby, either in wild conditions if you're in a rural area, or in the neighbour's gardens?

Rhododendrons, camellias and azaleas growing in an area indicate that the soil is acid. Houses built from local materials such as flint and limestone occur in areas with alkaline soils.

But the use of a soil testing kit is a sure way of establishing the levels in your own garden. The pH scale is a method of conveying how acid or alkaline a soil is; it ranges from 1 to 14, with 7 being neutral. Below this the soil is acidic, whereas from 7 to 14 it will be alkaline. Most plants prefer a soil that is 6.5 on the scale (nearly neutral), and it is unusual to find soils outside the range of 4–8.

EVALUATING THE LIGHT

Which Direction does your Garden Face?

A good way to tell the direction your garden faces without a compass is to remember the sun always rises in the east and sets in the west, so if the sun is on your left in the early morning you will be facing south. You need to know this in order to understand which parts of the garden will get the sun as it moves through the day. A wall facing due south will be sunny and sheltered for most of the day; if it faces west it will get the warm late afternoon sun, but be shaded in the morning; east facing walls get the cooler morning sun and can take a while to warm up; while north facing walls will get very little sun through the day and will be shaded and cool. The direction of the wind will also affect the temperature, depending on whether it is blowing from a warm or cold land or sea.

In winter the days are shorter with less daylight, and the sun does not get as high in the sky. In the height of summer the sun will be overhead at midday and the days will be longer. This can make it difficult to judge correctly how sunny a garden gets in the middle of winter when the sun may not reach parts of the garden at all. Equally, a garden with lots of deciduous trees may seem lighter in winter without the tree canopy and quite shady in summer due to the leaves blocking out the sun.

Full Sun or Semi Shade?

Of course, daylight is relevant to any aspect of garden design and particularly a planting scheme, but evaluating it is not always so straightforward. Fully understanding the light levels in all areas of your garden is essential to choosing the right plants. There are various terms used when referring to gardens and

Winter sunlight.

Poppies need full sun or the plants will grow leggy with fewer flowers.

plants such as 'full sun or 'semi shade'. What do these terms really mean? How much light does 'full sun' equate to? What denotes deep shade and what is the relevance when choosing plants?

Full sun means just that: daylight all day long, not just for a few hours in the morning or afternoon. Imagine a field with nothing but grass in it. The centre of the field receives full sun or daylight throughout the day. If the field has trees on its boundaries the areas where the trees cast a shadow do not receive full sun, but are in 'part shade'. The shorter the days and the lower the sun gets in the sky the longer the shadows will be and even more of the field will be in part shade.

In a garden, particularly a small garden, full sun can be difficult to achieve, and even in a large garden there are usually trees, shrubs or structures creating shade. The problem with growing sun-loving plants in anything less than full sun is they will not perform so well. They will become 'leggy' as they grow towards the light, with long weak stems which are more likely to fall over or require staking. They will probably produce fewer flowers and be more prone to pests and disease.

Plants which have adapted to semi shade, for example those living on the edge of woodland, will cope well with just a few hours of dappled sunlight during the day. Deep shade means no sunlight at all, but again there are plenty of plants which have adapted to these conditions even if they are not the most showy or colourful. A boring healthy plant will always look better than a sickly 'crowd pleaser'.

ASSESSING MOISTURE LEVELS

How wet or dry a garden is can also be quite difficult to evaluate, because it isn't so obvious by just looking at the soil. An open sunny part of the garden will probably be dryer than in a shady corner, but even digging down a few centimetres doesn't give us the full picture. The amount of moisture the ground can hold depends on the type of soil in the garden. Heavy clay will hold more and sandy soil will hold less.

The height of the water table in your area could also have a big impact on moisture levels. All ground has a water table, which can be many metres down or just a few centimetres below the surface, and in most cases this changes seasonally through the year, depending on the amount of rainfall. After a few months of no rain the water table can go down significantly, or a long period of heavy rain can bring the water table up close to the surface. Digging a hole is one way to look for the water table in your garden, but your local council or planning office should also have this information.

If you live in an area with a very high water table this will dramatically affect the moisture content of your soil and will determine which plants you can grow.

Plants which like very dry conditions will not thrive if their roots are wet for long periods; however, thirsty plants like hydrangea and willow will love it. Ground with a high water table for most of the year can be difficult to drain as the water has nowhere to be drained off to; in this case building raised planting beds is the only solution for any drought tolerant plants you wish to grow.

Existing plants, walls and buildings will also affect the moisture levels in a garden. The ground under trees, large shrubs and hedges tends to be dry because the plants are taking up the moisture. The ground at the bottom of a wall can be dry because it is sheltered from the rain. These places are also usually shady, giving rise to the term 'dry shade', which is most gardeners' least favourite conditions.

If there are no physical signs on the ground of the

Few gardens can tolerate flooding for long.

Wind turbulence can be caused by an impenetrable wall.

Bent trees in a garden on the coast.

moisture content in the soil, looking at which plants grow locally will give you clues. Willows, rhododendron, hydrangea and large-leaved perennials are a good indication that water is present and pine, buddleia, gorse and thyme would indicate very dry soil.

PROVIDING SHELTER FROM EXPOSURE

Gardens hate strong winds. More than drought, rain or frost, wind can do more damage to plants by drying out leaves, battering them down to the ground and breaking branches and stems. Fragile roots can be damaged by plants being rocked in the ground, particularly trees and shrubs. Some of the hardest types of country to create a garden in are open wind-swept plains or coastal regions with howling gales. These are extreme conditions, but nearly all gardens are susceptible to damage from strong winds. Sometimes this is due to air turbulence, which can be created when wind hits solid barriers such as walls and fences. In towns and cities wind tunnels are common between buildings.

Growing plants that have adapted to these conditions is sometimes the only solution, but there are many ways to protect against damage. Shelter breaks that use tough hedging or trees, such as rows of tall poplars, are a common site in open farmland. Use open trellis work or deciduous hedges instead of solid fencing and walls. Vulnerable plants can be protected in winter by wrapping them in horticultural fleece or even pruned stems, branches and leaves. Staking can prevent rocking, and regularly tying in climbing plants and wall shrubs will help, in addition to the use of plant supports. Grow plants with smaller leaves that will not get torn in the wind – think of pictures of bananas and palms after a hurricane.

All the practical information you can gather about the climate and weather in your area will help you understand the growing conditions in your garden. This will also help you to know what you can grow and, possibly more importantly, what you can't grow.

With a garden plan and study or site analysis, you can now look at the style you would like the planting to have.

FINDING THE RIGHT STYLE FOR YOUR GARDEN

Relating your garden to the local environment, looking at various garden styles, suiting the style to the location and function in the garden

Bold planting in a small garden.

Style describes how something is done or expressed. Most gardens have developed a particular style simply because of their location, size or function. An informal style, for example, may be the result of a family garden in a rural setting, which has a large area of

OPPOSITE PAGE: **A focal point in a simple green meadow.**

lawn surrounded by robust planting. In terms of style and general appearance your garden may look perfectly adequate, but it is unlikely to be making the best use of the space or getting the most out of its attributes. Opportunities may be missed by failing to draw attention to a lovely view or by having a limited selection of plants. Choosing a particular style is also a chance for the owners to express something of themselves in the garden.

RELATING YOUR GARDEN TO THE LOCAL ENVIRONMENT

A successful garden has a sense of place. This term describes an intangible characteristic that is present in beautiful outdoor spaces. It is used by designers to describe a garden that successfully connects with the character of its local environment. Like many architects, Frank Lloyd Wright was an advocate of this theory, and used it for example to integrate boulders already present on the site into one of his famous buildings, a family home in Pennsylvania. This sums up the best approach to choosing a style: the garden should be incorporated into the surroundings without imposing itself on them.

Rural locations can be more limiting when choosing a style, especially if there is a background view of countryside which will make exotic planting look out of place. In an urban situation where there may not be a definite character to the area, the chosen style can be more flexible. Tree ferns and bamboo don't look out of place if they have a courtyard wall as a backdrop, but will look out of place in a quintessential English rural setting. The type of plants that are appropriate to the

conditions in your garden will grow and thrive there because of the underlying geology. Rhododendrons and azaleas growing in woodland areas with acid soils look appropriate because they are growing in the right place surrounded by compatible plants.

The style should also be appropriate to the type of house that it surrounds, so that the garden and building relate to each other. Remember to take into consideration the interior of the house too, reinforcing the style in both areas. This is particularly relevant where there are large windows or glass doors merging the garden and interior together, and the view is clearly seen from both areas. A style of planting that reflects its surroundings will be more enduring than one that is inflicted on it.

As well as relating to its surroundings, the style should also reflect the personality and character of the owners. The decision may be easy when you are naturally drawn to a particular style and it fulfils all the above criteria. However, before using an idea that you may have seen elsewhere and wish to replicate in your own garden give it some consideration: does it really reflect your taste and situation? When the idea originates from a country that has a different climate

Willow sculptures reflect the rural setting.

A peaceful green and white garden.

and architecture, the result may be a sad imitation that doesn't relate to its surroundings in this country or its owners.

If ideas don't readily spring to mind, take some time to consider your own personal taste and the surroundings before a decision is made. Use the information you have gathered (described in the previous chapter) and supplement it with pictures of gardens, furniture and sculpture; you may surprise yourself as you see your true style emerging.

The style of a garden is emphasized not only by the type of plants that are used but also the manner in which they are grown and maintained. A yew hedge with crisp, neat lines represents formality by its strong colour and solidness; whereas a semi-evergreen hornbeam hedge that's cut to a soft, rounded outline will infer informality and make a semi-transparent boundary. The style is further reinforced by the principle of unity, where plant containers, furniture and all the other elements used in the garden are in the chosen style. The most successful gardens are those with an idea that is carried through the whole garden with confidence and clarity.

GARDEN STYLES

Formal

A formal style of gardening usually has straight lines and a clipped tidy appearance using shapes that have a geometric pattern and are symmetrical. Clipped hedges and topiary are representative of this style; topiary can be used in pairs to emphasize entrances or at the corner of rectangles or squares to highlight the geometry of the layout. Plants are often used differently in other parts of the world; clipped azalea in Japan represents mountains. When clipped in this way they are unable to flower, but are valued for their shape and form rather than colour.

Plants with small leaves, such as box, can be clipped to give a crisp outline, whilst larger-leaved specimens cannot and will therefore have a softer outline. Examples of plants used for topiary are: *Lonicera nitida*, bay, rosemary and yew. Fruit trees can be pruned into formal shapes such as espalier, cordon and fan. Classic roses and herbs such as sage and bay are also commonly used in formal gardens.

Neat straight lines create formality in a contemporary garden.

Natural

This style blends well into many settings. Plants are chosen for a relaxed natural habit of growth, and the layout is informal with curves rather than straight lines. A rural, informal style of planting is deceptively tricky and needs careful planning to be successful. The key is to ensure that there is some structure within the planting scheme, such as neat, clipped hedges, timber edging to lawns or topiarized plants, to prevent it looking messy.

Cottage Garden

The approach to cottage garden planting is very similar to the natural style, with perhaps less structure. Fruit and vegetables are traditionally integrated into the planting scheme. This type of garden requires a higher level of maintenance than many others. Unlike other styles of planting it relies on a diverse mix of plants, but for success it should always be underpinned by shrubs with strong formal shapes, such as neatly clipped box balls or holly, that always has a strong presence.

Japanese

The Japanese style creates a beautiful, contemplative garden. It has been used successfully in small courtyard areas of hospitals and colleges, where the calm atmosphere is very welcome. If you are considering using this style in your garden, give it a great deal of thought before making the decision. It can be difficult to integrate into most of our outside spaces because it doesn't easily relate to the European style of architecture and unfortunately can end up as a pastiche of the style.

Genuine Japanese gardens place elements such as lanterns, water features and stones with great significance in a manner that has developed over many years.

A mown path through long grass.

Typical Rural Garden Plants

Shrubs

- Corylus (hazel)
- Fuchsia (small-flowered types)
- Ilex (holly)
- Osmanthus
- Philadelphus
- Roses
- Sambucus (elderberry)
- Syringa (lilac)
- Clipped and topiary shrubs (such as box and yew) for a structural element

Herbaceous perennials

- Aster and other plants with daisy-like flowers
- Digitalis (foxglove)
- Geranium (cranesbill)
- Lupin
- Peony
- Primula
- Salvia
- Viola

A more successful approach for European gardens is to adopt a more diluted version of the style in its simplest form, using as few elements as possible. Plants with japonica in their name are obviously a good choice, as this denotes that they originate from this part of the world. Flower and colour are less important than shape, form and simplicity. Structural plants such as neatly clipped box, azalea, pines, Japanese maples and bamboo are more representative of this style. Adopting the discipline of having a more reduced

Bamboo creates an oriental atmosphere.

> **Typical Mediterranean Plants**
>
> - Pines
> - *Cupressus sempervirens* (pencil cypress)
> - *Acacia dealbata* (mimosa)
> - *Campsis radicans* (trumpet vine)
> - *Chamaerops humilis* (fan palm)
> - *Vitis vinefera* (grapevine)
> - Lavender
> - Olive
> - Oleander (beware as these are poisonous)
> - Herbs (such as rosemary, thyme and sage), which are wonderfully ornamental as well as useful

number of species than we would usually want to use will result in the most successful result.

Mediterranean

The Mediterranean garden is a popular style for urban areas, probably because a more sheltered environment is available, although many Mediterranean plants, such as olive trees, are used to freezing winter conditions. This style lends itself to urban backdrops, whereas many typically Mediterranean plants look rather alien against a British rural setting. These plants depend on a well-drained soil and will not survive in heavy clay soil, though if you have these conditions in your garden you could grow them in containers where you can control the soil type to suit the plant.

Meadow

Meadows or areas of meadow create atmospheric naturalistic spaces in a garden. It's not necessary to have a large area of land; a small strip at the end of a garden, especially if the outlook is a rural view, is an effective transitional method of joining more formal areas to informal ones. Meadows need light and sun to grow well, and are not simply areas of grass left to grow wild – you will need to do some research to establish which plants will grow in the particular soil and aspect of your garden.

Wildlife Garden

A wildlife garden used to be thought of as a rather informal style, where plants would be left to their own devices and nature would eventually take over. This discouraged some gardeners who prefer a tidy appearance to their gardens. However the reality is that it's a style of gardening that can be incorporated into any type of garden, be it formal or informal, and has enormous benefits.

Wildlife gardening encourages biodiversity by using a range of plants, including pollen and nectar rich flowers, that attract a range of beneficial creatures such as birds, bees and other insects. This creates a balanced chain of wildlife that is self-supporting, so that pests such as aphids and slugs are eaten by predators. So think of creating habitats for visitors to your garden, encouraging them to stay and breed, and try to avoid using chemicals that upset the balance.

The advantage is that as gardeners we can use beneficial wildlife in balance to keep pests to

Bees prefer flowers with an open structure.

a minimum: the birds eat caterpillars, slugs and aphids; frogs and toads eat slugs; bats eat insects; and hedgehogs eat slugs. As a result our plants will be healthier and more productive; garden maintenance is reduced when there are fewer pests and diseases to deal with; the environment is improved when fewer chemicals are used; and we have more time to enjoy the results.

Choose appropriate plants for the conditions in your garden so they will need minimal intervention to remain healthy, and use disease-resistant varieties of plants where possible. Climbing plants make nesting and roosting sites; nectar-rich, bee-friendly plants such as honeysuckle and ivy are valuable because they produce nectar-rich flowers followed by fruits. Flowers such as *Limnanthes douglasii* (poached egg plant) with a simple open structure are attractive to most insects. Encourage insects such as ladybirds, hoverflies, and lacewings that will eat pests such as greenfly.

To avoid the use of chemicals, where necessary use biological controls to control pests; for example, the nematode that predates vine weevil is far more effective than any chemical treatments. Have at least one compost heap depending on the size of your garden, a decorative one in a small garden or two or three in a larger one.

Wildlife Garden Plants

Trees

Alnus glutinosa (alder)   Cones attract finches and siskins

Betula pendula (birch)   Supports many insects that attract birds

Quercus robur (oak)   Supports a variety of insects eaten by birds; the acorns are eaten by wood pigeons and great spotted woodpeckers

Fagus sylvatica (beech)   Nuts are eaten by tits, chaffinches, great spotted woodpeckers and nuthatches

Shrubs

Cotoneaster   Good cover and berries for birds; bees like the flowers

Pyracantha   Birds prefer the variety that produces red berries

Lavender   Butterflies and bees like the flowers

Privet   Birds like the black berries

Climbing Plants

Lonicera periclymenum (honeysuckle)   Flowers attract bees and moths; the berries attract birds

Ivy   Good for nesting; flowers attract insects in autumn

Herbaceous Plants

The following provide fruit and seeds that attract garden birds:

Helianthus annus   (sunflower)

Aster novi-belgii   (michaelmas daisy)

Oenothera species   (evening primrose)

Centaura cyanus   (cornflower)

Limnanthes douglessi   (poached egg plant)

We all enjoy the sound of birdsong in our gardens, and birds are valuable to us for eating pests such as slugs and snails. Provide a variety of foods to attract different types of birds that will eat a range of pests. Put up bird boxes to attract birds into the garden; use different sizes and types of box to ensure that a good range of birds will use them. Provide a home for other small creatures by creating a small pond or water feature. If children use the garden, fill the pond with pebbles or cover it with a custom-made special grid.

SUITING STYLE TO LOCATION

Courtyard

There is a lot of scope for different planting styles in courtyard gardens, as they are enclosed spaces without the surroundings and variety of architecture that constrain most other forms of planting design. A minimal or Japanese style can more easily be integrated into these spaces than elsewhere. There are also opportunities to be creative with form and colour: the walls could be painted with strong colours as a backdrop to show off the shapes of plants, creating a striking scenario. If the courtyard can be seen at night from rooms within the house, think about up-lighting certain plants or small trees with strong shapes to create interesting shadows.

Courtyards are usually small spaces with lower light levels; this is where the restrictions about what can be planted will apply. Monitor the conditions of the area before you decide what plants to use and notice how much light is available, remembering that this will vary at different times of the year. Use this information to help you draw up a list of suitable plants.

All plants in a small space are visible and must be carefully chosen; a simplified approach is usually best – be disciplined and restrict the number of species. Choose three or four types of plants that suit the conditions, depending on the size of the area, and use multiples of them. The smaller the plant, the more of them can be used. Use fewer numbers of bigger plants such as shrubs, and probably only one small tree if there is room.

Getting it right first time isn't always easy due to poor light and inadequate rainfall; be prepared to monitor the plants regularly and edit where necessary.

Front Garden

Unlike the rest of the garden, the front garden is used on most days of the year as we enter and leave the house and is viewed from inside the house. The entrance to our house is important because it gives a

Bin storage in a stylish front garden.

Sempervivum **thrive in well-drained conditions.**

first impression of the house and what may be found inside; estate agents call it kerb appeal. Despite this, front gardens can be neglected spaces. Most are quite small in relation to the rest of the garden, but they have a number of functions, often providing a parking space for at least one car and storing dustbins and recycling boxes. The need for planted areas in front gardens to absorb rainwater and help prevent flooding, resulted in the 2008 legislation that requires planning permission if more than five square meters of impermeable paving is used.

Small areas of planting can provide an area of garden that is filled with dynamism and interest. By choosing plants imaginatively, you can return home on a winter evening to the sweet scent of *Sarcococca* (Christmas box), a small easily maintained evergreen shrub with highly scented white flowers in late winter, or enjoy spring flowering daffodils and tulips. Where space is tight, wall shrubs and climbing plants are a good solution to provide more opportunities for planting and are useful planted against trellis to screen dustbins. Dense plantings of *Pyracantha* (fire-thorn) or holly can also be used at boundaries to deter intruders.

Roof Garden or Balcony

A roof garden or balcony presents the opportunity to create a garden in cities and urban spaces where outdoor space is usually at a premium. All the plants are in containers, and compost can be manipulated to give a wider variety of growing conditions, increasing the choice of plants that are available. It is a specialized environment that requires careful planning and planting because its position makes it very exposed to the elements. The type of plants chosen depends on the size of the garden and how much shelter there is; a more sheltered environment allows a wider variety of plants to be used in this situation.

Creating screens, such as trellis panels, will filter wind and create a little shade; glass panels can be used to preserve a lovely view if you are lucky enough to have one. Any boundary structures must be semi-permeable to allow a certain amount of wind through, to prevent turbulence. If you are unsure, consult a garden designer or landscape contractor who will be able to advise on the most appropriate type of boundary treatment.

It is impossible to give a definitive list of plants for a roof garden or balcony, because of the variability of conditions and the location. Exposure to sun and wind are the main problems, so choose plants that have adapted to tough conditions, such as those grown in coastal regions or hot Mediterranean climates. Avoid using large-leaved plants such as *Tracycarpus fortunei* and bananas, as their leaves will shred in high winds.

Choose appropriate plants that will withstand the dry conditions and do not need extra irrigation to coax them along once they are established. Silver leaves are a good indicator, as they usually have a covering of tiny hairs that protect them, such as *Stachys byzantina* (lamb's ears). Plants that have leaves with a waxy surface that reduces moisture loss or small narrow leaves also survive well in these tough conditions. Some Mediterranean plants, such as lavender, rosemary and cistus (rock-rose) release essential oils to protect them from hot sun; we can also enjoy the wonderful aroma that is released in this process. Using compost that is a 50:50 mix of multi-purpose and a loam-based compost (such as John Innes) will retain water and allow plants to take up moisture gradually.

Plants and their containers, especially when wet, are very heavy so it is essential to make sure that the roof or balcony space is load-bearing. Consult a structural engineer to ensure that no damage will be done to the building by the extra weight.

RELATING STYLE TO FUNCTION

Water Features

Water features are an endless source of fascination for adults and children. The wide range available from a small kit-form wall mask and basin to a large pond can be accommodated in any garden. The tinkling sound of water in a wall-mounted feature creates a restful atmosphere, and a pond can create

A smart water feature in a small garden.

Aquatic Plants
Marginal Plants
Acorus calamus (sweet flag) *Caltha palustris* (kingcups) *Equisetum scirpoides*   Small vertical, bamboo-like stem *Gunnera manicata*   Very large plant with rhubarb-like leaves
Deep Water Plants
Aponogeton distachyos (water hawthorn) *Nymphaea* (waterlilies)   Available in various sizes and colours

a calm reflective surface. A pond in the garden provides an opportunity for a broader range of plants, which will help to keep water clear and free of algal growth. Even small ponds can attract wildlife,

providing somewhere for birds and other wildlife to drink, bathe and feed.

All water features require a certain amount of annual maintenance depending on their size, so consider this carefully when deciding how to incorporate one into the garden. Care must be taken if small children use the garden, even if only on an occasional basis.

Green Roofs

A green roof has a planting of grass or other plants over a waterproof membrane. Their recent popularity stems mainly from the consequences of climate change that have seen a cycle of flooding and droughts in recent years. They reduce water run-off by absorbing up to 60 per cent of rainwater that falls on the roof. The natural insulation properties retain the building's heat in winter; and they help to keep the building cool as the plants absorb heat in hot weather and do not radiate it back into the atmosphere, thus reducing the surrounding air temperature. They provide a valuable

A chamomile green roof.

habitat for wildlife, no matter how small the area that is covered.

Turf has been used over roofs in Scandinavia for centuries. In our climate there is a wider range of plants available, such as sedum for sunny areas or small ferns and shade loving plants where there is less light. The plants should have fibrous roots, rather than single long taproots, and should require little or no irrigation and need little maintenance. A green roof is more expensive to install than a conventional roof. Professional installation is recommended because there are serious issues about the extra weight and the correct waterproofing over the roof surface.

Living Walls

A living wall consists of special plant-filled modules that are fixed to an upright wall. Like the green roofs, living walls retain winter heat in a building and cool surrounding air in summer. They also offer sound absorption and create a vibrant green look in a city. There are some wonderful examples on commercial buildings. However, as a domestic feature, they are expensive to install, and require quite a lot of maintenance and irrigation to keep them looking good.

A living wall.

Rain Gardens

A rain garden is a depression created to collect and store rainwater running from impermeable surfaces (such as asphalt, concrete and block paving), then allowing it slowly to soak into the ground. Any area of garden can be formed into a rain garden. The depressions can be located along the edge of a driveway or a larger area at a low point in the garden. It can be planted with suitable plants to help slow the run-off, or gravel and cobbles can be used as decorative features. There may be a gravel-filled trench below it to increase the storage capacity and allow water to soak into the ground more easily. Rain gardens are widely used in the USA and elsewhere but are a relatively new concept in the UK.

Fruit and Vegetables

There has been a lot more interest in growing fruit and vegetables in our gardens during the last few years. They can be incorporated into the garden either as a practical vegetable plot or grown in containers if space is an issue. Most fruit and vegetables are attrac-

tive as well as functional; purple sage, rosemary and chives look as good as any ornamental plant in a border.

Trained fruit trees can be incorporated to be both ornamental and productive. Apples and pears can be grown as cordons – a single main stem at an angle of 45 degrees – that take up very little room and yet still produce a quantity of fruit. Grown on a dwarfing root stock, they require simple pruning twice a year.

A vegetable potager is a style of growing vegetables that not only looks attractive, so it can take centre stage in a garden, but it's also productive. A traditional potager has a formal design, with a grid of paths and beds using geometric shapes such as rectangles, squares and diamonds to create the layout. Herbs and edible flowers are also incorporated with vegetables to create a visually appealing design.

Using Scent in the Garden

Scent is often overlooked when choosing plants, but it can have a powerful effect in the garden, evoking strong memories and emotions. Herbs can remind us of food, and other scents may remind us of childhood

Tomatoes growing in a hanging basket.

A greenhouse increases the possibilities of what can be grown.

memories and events. Scent is present in a wide range of plants from the sweet perfume of roses to the heady smell of lilies, but it is not just flowers that convey scent; leaves such as rosemary and lavender have essential oils in their leaves that are released by the warmth of the sun.

Scents evoke a different response depending on the situation and time of year. The heady scent of a rose can be a great pleasure in the warm weather, whilst winter scent in a garden can be unexpected, but always a welcome and uplifting experience. To create the most effective atmosphere, place scented plants strategically where they will be enjoyed – pot of lilies next to a seating area for example, or lavender hedges lining a path so that they release their scent as you brush against it.

Containers

Growing plants in containers is the ideal solution for plants that aren't suitable for the natural conditions in the garden. Smaller varieties of Japanese maples, for example, grow happily in containers where acid soil is not available in the garden; vegetables can be nourished in rich compost; and plants that scorch in sunshine can be grown in containers in a shady part of a paved garden.

Containers are ideal for plants that define the seasons, such as spring planting of bulbs and shrubs with autumn colour. Ring the changes and prevent things looking static by siting a planted container, performing at its peak, to be seen from a window in the house. This needs some planning, so ensure that you have containers waiting in the wings ready to take centre stage. Different varieties of tulips have many months of successional flowering, and pelargoniums flower for weeks if they are dead-headed regularly.

Containers provide an opportunity to have some fun trying different colour combinations and shapes; if they work, the ideas can be used in more permanent planting in the garden.

Contemporary planted containers.

WORKING WITH COLOUR

What is colour? Colour in nature, the effect of light levels, creating a colour scheme, combining colours, working with natural materials

Primary colours red, yellow and blue.

WHAT IS COLOUR?

Definitions of colour go back hundreds of years, and each society's association with colour can vary from others around the globe. Colour can be complex and confusing to work with, and it is still largely a mystery how our brains interpret the colours we see around us. Why does one person like yellow flowers and another hate them? Is it because their brains are interpreting the colour differently, or do they have different associations? The plants grown by our

OPPOSITE PAGE: *Echinops ritro* (Globe thistle).

parents and grandparents can have a strong effect on our likes and dislike as adults. Some people love the flowers from their childhood, but others may associate them with unhappy visits to an ageing relative.

Today's gardener is also a designer with a discerning eye. They know what they like, but it can be frustratingly difficult to achieve what they have in mind with plants. While artists and printers can mix paint or ink to create an exact colour, there is less control using plants in a palette, so understanding how colours work together and the atmosphere they can project is essential when painting with plants.

How We See Colour

We can see colour because of light waves moving through the atmosphere, and the human eye is sensitive to a certain range of these waves called visible light. When these waves are split, for example through a prism, we see colours known as the colour spectrum, which are also the colours we see in a rainbow. The six pure spectral colours visible to the human eye are violet, blue, green, yellow, orange and red. When light waves hit an object it will absorb some of these spectral colours and reflect others. It is these reflected colours that we see. An apple is red because red is the only colour not to be absorbed by it; therefore we see it as red.

COLOUR IN NATURE

Colour occurs in nature for many different reasons: for example, plants and animals are coloured to attract or protect, warn or camouflage; and minerals in rocks form colours due to chemical reactions with air and water.

Adaptation and genetic evolution play a role when living organisms use colour to survive and flourish, such as flowers and berries which have evolved to attract pollinators and seed distributors. The unripe holly berry is green, hidden against the plant's foliage; only when they are ready to be eaten do they turn red and stand out against the dark green leaves. So when growing plants for their ornamental berries, bear in mind that the red berries are usually eaten first, while the yellow or white berries of sorbus for example are left longer on the tree.

The colours of flowers have evolved to send signals to insects. Some plants have inconspicuous flowers that lure night-pollinating insects with scent as a signal rather than colour. For example *Elaeagnus ebbingii* has very small, pale yellow flowers, but their smell will reach you before you can even see the plant itself.

Leaves however appear green because they contain food producing chlorophyll pigments which absorb light energy during the process of photosynthesis. Chlorophylls are pigments that reflect green light while they absorb red, yellow, blue and violet from the colour spectrum; therefore we see green when we look at leaves. When this chlorophyll pigment decays due to cold, other pigments then appear which were concealed by the green chlorophylls and we get the yellow, orange and red of autumn showing through.

A wildflower meadow has a simple harmony and balance of colour.

Variegated leaves occur when areas on a leaf have less or no chlorophyll pigment; this is an accident in nature. Plants with variegated leaves will grow slower than their plain-leaved varieties due to less food producing chlorophyll, and in the wild they would either revert back to their original form or be outgrown by stronger competitors.

THE EFFECT OF LIGHT LEVELS ON COLOUR

Changing Light through the Day

Time does not stand still, and the light levels in a garden are constantly changing as the sun moves across the sky. As a result colours appear to change throughout the day and night. Early morning light is soft and mellow with a yellow tinge, which makes yellows and lime greens glow. At mid day in the height of summer when the sun is full, colour can appear diluted, whereas in late afternoon the light has more orange in it and bright colours will sing out with intensity. Most garden photographers prefer working in the early morning or late afternoon when the colours are more saturated.

As we know, at night the world is drained of colour; this is due to the receptors in our eyes which require more light to work. Bright colours will appear grey and can be indistinguishable from each other. Even electric light cannot give definition to strong colours, and this should be taken into account when choosing plants for a garden which will be used at night. White flowers and stems or pale leaves will reflect what light there is and stand out far more than strong reds or blues which will pretty much disappear. In low light levels our eyes are most sensitive to the colour green.

Light and Different Climates

How we see colour is dependant on the quality of natural light. In hot climates the intense light levels saturate colours and diminish them, whereas in cooler climates with lower light levels the opposite happens and colours appear richer and more vibrant. Bright pink bougainvillea, much loved across the Mediterranean, will scream out in the soft light of the North, and the same is true of the many plants we use from South Africa, which survive only as annuals or summer bedding. Successfully combining flower colours which have evolved in stronger light conditions than our own takes a certain amount of skill and care.

Light through the Seasons

In the northern and southern hemispheres we have seasons where the light levels change through the year. In the extreme North and South, summer days last twenty-four hours, but winter nights are just as long. The nearer to the equator the extremes of seasons and light become less, with the length of winter being very similar to summer. These changes in light levels affect the way we see colour in a garden through the seasons.

In spring, when light levels are lower and there is less haze from the sun, colour can appear stronger than in the summer. Flowers which have a subtle glow in the spring and autumn may become overpowered in the harsh summer light. The bright green of emerging leaf buds which give spring and early summer that lovely fresh glow is aided by the soft yellow light of spring, and equally the fiery reds and oranges of autumn are emphasized by the amber light which accompanies the season. Winter has a pale yellow or grey light which can have a quality of its own, making winter flowering plants such a treat on a short cold day.

Shade from Buildings and Trees

Unless a garden is created from an open field, there is usually some shade from buildings, trees or large shrubs at some part of the day. In addition to shade impacting on the growing conditions it will also affect how the colours of flowers, leaves and bark appear. A

Hakonechloa macra 'Aureola' and *Clematis* 'Abundance'. Yellow-leaved plants brighten up gloomy corners.

dark corner can be brightened by using plants with light coloured leaves or bark, or using white flowers which stand out in the gloom. Yellow leaved plants work very well in less light, especially as they can scorch in strong sunlight and turn brown. *Philadelphus coronarius* 'Aurea' or *Choisya* 'Sundance', for example, are very effective in light shade. They may not have such a strong leaf colour as in full sun, especially later in the summer, but they will still be bright without brown scorch marks.

Sun-loving plants will struggle to produce flowers if they are grown in low light levels, so use plants which have adapted to light shade such as woodland plants. Many, such as azaleas, aquilegias and hydrangeas, will happily flower in dappled shade or just a couple of hours sun a day, preferring the cool moist conditions to full sun. Variegated plants can also work well; however, many variegated or strong-coloured leaves may lose their definition in very low light and almost revert back to green due to the plant needing green chlorophylls to produce food. As the pale areas of a variegated leaf contain less or no chlorophyll, the plant will try to revert back to green in order to survive.

CREATING A COLOUR SCHEME

Deciding on which colours to use in your garden can be confusing and challenging, but they should be part of the whole design and relate very much to the style of the garden. Designing plant colours in isolation is difficult, as they may also have to compliment other materials such as stone, timber or painted surfaces and this will be part of the overall design concept.

A colour scheme can remain the same from spring to winter, if you like, with just a slight shift through the seasons. On the other hand it can change radically, with perhaps bright yellow and green in spring going to fiery oranges and reds in the autumn. There is no need to worry about spring-flowering daffodils clashing with pink dahlias, because they will not be flowering at the same time. However if this seems a little overwhelming keep your scheme as simple as possible to begin with. The simplest schemes with fewer colour choices will always be more reliable and easier to achieve.

Choosing the Right Colours for the Job

Human emotions can be affected by the use of different colours to create a mood in a garden.

Green is the most popular colour and is the most restful on the eye; it can easily be seen over a distance, as shown by the green of traffic lights.

Blue can be calm and soothing, but may also represent cold and depression, with bright colours creating energy, lifting the spirits and leaping out of the picture.

Plants with blue and dark green will recede and appear further away, while bright reds, oranges and yellows will come towards you and stand out; this can be used to create a depth of field just with colour.

Too many different or clashing colours used together will create disharmony and look awkward, whereas simple colour schemes will always feel serene and harmonious.

The colour of the paint in this show garden is perfectly matched to *Crocosmia* **'Lucifer'.**

A good analogy is a piece of music: think of the whole garden as complete melody with a theme running through it; there will be repeated phrases, a chorus and maybe very loud and then very quiet sequences. What kind of garden do you want to create – will it be restful, happy, exciting or even melancholy? This kind of emotional association can help bring a scheme together, as each part of the garden will require a different theme. For example the entrance to the garden could be upbeat, with loud, bright colours giving way to a transition of quiet, simple greens leading to a calm seating area with pale pink, blue and grey. Then leaving that part of the garden you enter a large expanse of lawn, with strong explosive oranges and reds that sing out while you walk over to a dark entrance in a hedge. Through the hedge is a gloomy wood with glowing yellows and pale creams that create a discordant melody, unless it's spring before the tree canopy is formed, and the area is bright and happy with yellow erythronium, daffodils and blue-bells. The music can change through the seasons and even through the day. This idea of carrying a colour theme around a garden works just as well in a very small garden as in a large one; it's just a question of scale.

Overleaf are a few possible scenarios.

An area used for dining and entertaining: A sense of energy is created using rich reds and pinks against a green background.

A reception area such as a front garden: A simple but constantly changing scheme for all seasons.

A view from the kitchen window: Culinary herbs and seasonal salad vegetables with companion planting, roses and annuals.

A transition from one part of the garden to another: Subtle colours and textures which do not compete with nearby schemes.

A quiet place for reading and relaxing: A simple scheme with cool purple, pale pink and soft grey leaves, or even just green and white.

A natural woodland: A riot of greens, colourful stems and bark with seasonal blossom, berries and hips.

Colour Terminology

When someone asks for a different shade, do they mean a different colour or the same colour only lighter or darker? Should they really ask for a colour with a different intensity or a different hue? Colour terms have become part of our everyday language, sometimes misrepresented, but a basic under-standing of the terminology helps when working with and communicating about colour.

Hue   another name for colour
Tint   a colour diluted with white

Tone   a colour with black or grey added
Shade   what colour would look like if light were shaded from it
Key colour   the dominant colour in a colour scheme or mixture
Neutral grey   black and white mixed together
Intensity   the brightness or dullness of a colour
Primary colours   red, yellow and blue
Secondary colour   the result when two primary colours are mixed together: orange (red + yellow), green (blue + yellow) and violet (blue + red)

COMBINING COLOURS

The relationship people have with colour varies enor-mously; some find it a daily source of wonder, while others wonder what all the fuss is about. Some use it instinctively, while others struggle to understand it. However, human beings have been manipulating and using colour for thousands of years, and it has as much to do with science and physics as it does art. In the seventeenth century when Isaac Newton experi-mented with light and prisms and discovered spectral colours, art theorists of the time named red, yellow and blue the 'primary colours'. They believed that every known colour could be created from just these three, which is not strictly true, but it became a rec-ognized theory for understanding and manipulating colour in art which we still use today.

The Colour Wheel

Developed in the early eighteenth century, the colour wheel is still used today to help us organize and combine colours. It is made up of the primaries red, yellow and blue and shows what happens when these colours are mixed together. The wheel also helps to illustrate the different qualities colours have when they are put next to each other. For example

colours opposite each other on the wheel are called complimentary and create a vibrancy or contrast. Red is the complimentary colour of green, yellow is oppo-site violet, and blue is opposite orange. These colours will stand out if put together in a scheme, whereas colours next to each other on the wheel, such as red and orange or blue and green, will be harmonious.

The three primary colours, red, yellow and blue become more complex when other colours are

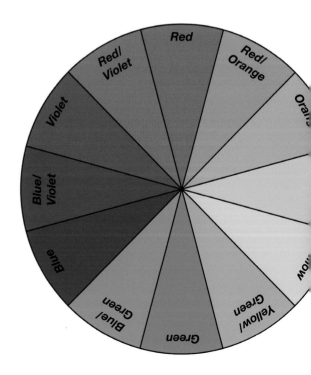

The colour wheel.

Apricot harmonizes with yellow because it contains yellow, whereas magenta clashes with yellow because it contains blue.

added. When a little yellow is mixed with red it becomes red/orange, and when a little blue is mixed with red it becomes red/violet. If these colours are then diluted with white they both become pink, but one will have yellow in it and the other will be bluish. Both are still pink but with a subtle difference. A red/violet or magenta may clash with yellow because it contains blue, but the red/orange will be harmonious with yellow because it contains yellow. Most colours can be dissected to find their origins in red, yellow or blue, and understanding this theory allows greater manipulation and creativity when working with colour.

WORKING WITH NATURAL MATERIALS

Because the range of colours found in the plant world is infinite and unpredictable, working with colour in the garden can be exciting but also frustrating. By choosing a colour scheme, you have begun to limit the huge list of plants available. Whilst this will make it much easier to make the final decision about what to use, nature has a way of imposing its own random influences on our carefully thought out ideas. Sometimes this can be delightful and other times plain annoying, so this is another good reason to keep the scheme simple to begin with.

Accidents often happen, whether it's a wrongly labelled plant, the unpredictable effect of growing conditions or a self-seeded impostor, and a decision is needed to go with the accident or not. When this

A colour swatch showing some of the many colours found in the leaves and stems of plants, which can be used to create a canvas.

happens you are making a design decision: does the impostor fit in with the colour scheme, does it add to it or detract, and would it be better moved to another part of the garden? When people say their wonderful planting scheme just happened by accident with no planning, they are being modest about their ability to work with and modify accidents. The artistic skill

is in knowing when to interfere and when to leave alone. Watercolour painting is often described as a series of controlled accidents, and planting design is very similar.

Some plants have long flowering seasons, such as hardy geraniums and roses, but many others are very fleeting, as with peonies and poppies. Flowers are the

Plants and their seasons.

	Spring	Summer	Autumn	Winter
Red				
Yellow				
Blue				
Green				
Violet				
Pink				
Orange				
White				

ephemeral, ornamental elements in a garden, constantly changing or disappearing, so relying purely on flowers to create a colour scheme is very limiting. It is possible, however, to create a scheme which has colour all year round by just using leaves, stems and bark, and there is a huge variety of colours. They can be used very successfully on their own, creating a strong canvas which will be more durable through the year, and any flowers will be a bonus rather than a necessity.

Colour Board

A colour board is a useful tool when looking for creative inspiration. It allows you to experiment with ideas freely. To make one, gather together objects you like, basing your choice purely on their colours – a favourite painting, a ball of wool, even a tea cup. Arrange them together and take a photograph to keep for reference. Alternatively collect images of plants or ideas from magazines, catalogues and printed off the internet and stick them down on a large piece of paper or card.

Once you have a selection of colours which work well together you are ready to convert them into items for the garden – flowers, leaves, stems or bark. Choosing only those plants which suit the growing conditions in your garden make a list of plants you would like to include, using the colours on your board. Ensure that you include something for each season.

Because colour is subjective and emotive it can be a powerful tool in garden design. Colour can be both a delight and a frustration but so can any form of creativity, especially when working with natural ingredients. Nature will always throw in some unexpected results – it's what you do with them that counts.

The next stage looks at the role plants play in forming and defining the garden, giving it a solid workable structure for the ornamental elements.

The Sample Border

The colour board is used to help create a design brief, along with all the other criteria such as growing conditions, planting style and function. You can then begin choosing plants which fit the design brief. A scenario for a border has been created to show how the process works, and this will be followed through in Chapter 6 to create a planting plan.

The Brief

The soil in the garden is a well-drained sandy loam with a neutral pH and the border is sheltered from the wind and sunny for most of the day. The position of the border is next to the kitchen door and can be seen from inside the house so needs to look good all year. The planting needs to include some herbs for cooking, and the style should be naturalistic with some strong dramatic shapes. The colour scheme should be pretty but sophisticated using soft greys and greens with yellow, purple and white flowers, but maybe some dark leaves for a bit drama.

Season	Trees	Climbing & Wall Shrubs	Evergreen Shrubs	Deciduous Shrubs	Evergreen Perennials, Ferns and Grasses	Deciduous Perennials, Ferns and Grasses	Annuals or Biennials	Seasonal Bulbs
Spring	Amelanchier lamarckii	Clematis alpina Ceanothus 'Italian Skies' Clematis montana 'grandiflora'	Myrtus communis Magnolia stellata Rosemary officinalis	Deutzia gracilis Spirea 'Arguta' Syringa vulgaris 'Charles Joly' Elaeagnus 'Quicksilver'	Epimedium x youngianum 'Niveum'	Iris 'Sable' Iris pallida 'Variegata' Pulmonaria officinalis 'Sissinghurst White'	Cerinthe major Aquilegia alpina	Tulip 'Spring Green' Daffodil 'Tete-à-Tete'
Summer	Cornus kousa 'China Girl'	Rose climbing 'Iceberg' Clematis 'Alba Luxurians Clematis 'Perle d'Azur' Trachelospermum jasminoides	Lavender 'Hidcote' Ceanothus 'Autumn Blue' Cistus x corbariensis Salvia officinalis Convolvulus cneorum	Philadelphus coronarius 'Variegatus' Rosa 'Glamis Castle' Rosa 'Graham Thomas' White Hibiscus Perovskia 'Blue Spire'	Stachys byzantina 'Big Ears Libertia 'grandiflora'	Pennisetum orientale Centaurea montana Dianthus 'Mrs Sinkins' Eryngium alpinum Geranium himalayense Kniphofia 'Little Maid' Lychnis coronaria 'Alba'	Convolvulus sabatius	Lilium regale
Autumn		Passiflora caerulea 'Constance Elliot' Parthenocissus henryana	Hebe 'Autumn Glory' Buddleja davidii 'Empire Blue'	Perovskia 'Blue Spire'	Melianthus major Fuchsia 'Hawkshead'	Anemone x hybrida 'Honorine Jobert' Verbena bonariensis	Nicotiana sylvestris	Dahlia 'White Ballet'
Winter		Chaenomeles speciosa 'Nevalis' Garrya elliptica	Box balls Sarcococca humilis		Astelia chathamica			Snowdrops
All Year	Weeping Pear	Hedera helix 'Eva'	Euonymus fortunei 'Silver Queen' Choisya 'Aztec Pearl' Hebe albicans Osmanthus x burkwoodii Pittosporum 'Garnettii'		Cortaderia selloana 'Pumilla' Cotoneaster franchettii Astelia chathamica Helleborus argutifolius Lamium maculatum 'White Nancy'			

To help organize the list of plants which might be used, they have been put into a table showing the different plant categories and the seasons. The chosen plants fit the brief in terms of colour, and they are all compatible with the growing conditions in the garden.

THE ROLE OF PLANTS IN YOUR GARDEN

Creating a unified garden, using structural plants and ornamental plants, introducing scent, colour, shape and texture into the garden

Hedges, pleached trees and perennial plants are combined beautifully in this garden.

We all recognize that plants are the soft, colourful elements of any garden. They have a variety of roles to play: they can be dramatic and attention grabbing,

OPPOSITE PAGE: **A framework of hedges contain the ornamental planting.**

shy and retiring, a pleasing shape and colour that can be either soothing and restful, or brightly coloured, injecting energy into the garden.

We're used to using favourite plants for these characteristics, but they can have a much greater role to play.

The Role of Plants in the Garden

- Serve as focal points
- Provide structural elements
- Determine your route round the garden
- Give shade
- Add perfume and colour

- Remind us of the seasons
- Screen unwanted views
- Highlight favourable ones
- Create space and volume, preventing the garden from looking flat and uninteresting
- Provide us with fruit and vegetables, in their most fundamental, time-honoured role

Herbs and vegetables in a kitchen garden.

CREATING A UNIFIED GARDEN

It can be overwhelming to think about different types of planting for the whole garden. Initially it may seem easier to plan small areas of the garden in manageable sizes. However this often results in different parts of the garden that don't relate to each other and ends up comprising a rather random collection of plants that strike a note of discord rather than harmony.

The garden will be much more successful by starting with a plan of the whole area to work to (see Chapter 1). As you proceed, you'll expand your plant knowledge and learn more about the type of plants that grow well in your garden. Don't worry if you don't have an instinct for combining plants together; it's a skill that can be learned – though it is likely that there may be a certain amount of trial and error along the way if you're a complete beginner.

There can be challenges whatever the size of the garden. Many elements may need to be fitted into a

Soft green and white plants are used to edge the path contrasting with tightly clipped shrubs.

small garden, and every inch must work well because problems will be more apparent. On the other hand, there are also challenges when planting a large garden; it may be difficult to imagine how the space can be divided up and what plants will work well in all the different areas. Larger gardens often have more diverse areas of aspect and soil, so a greater knowledge of plants will be required.

The simplest and most effective method of choosing what role plants will play your garden is to divide them into roles as either structural or ornamental plants.

STRUCTURAL PLANTS

As the name suggests, structural plants are the main players in the composition of the garden. They provide the bones that will be visible in winter when many of the leaves and flowers of decorative plants are no longer there.

A border of ornamental plants and small structural grasses.

A black and white version clearly shows how structural planting works.

What Structural Plants Can Do

- Compartmentalize the garden
- Enclose areas for privacy
- Protect from the elements such as strong winds
- Provide a permanent structure
- Screen unattractive views
- Mark boundaries
- Announce entrances
- Serve as a backdrop for ornamental plants
- Encourage wildlife by providing nesting habitats
- Direct the flow around the garden
- Enhance the chosen style of the garden

Structural plants at the base of steps indicating a change in level.

Structural plants have many important uses in gardens. They can enclose areas or direct a route; they can even control the speed of movement around the garden. They are useful for screening some areas of the garden so that it won't be viewed all at once, or for allowing a filtered view to an adjoining area of the garden, creating a sense of mystery and persuading the visitor to explore further.

Key Plants

Key plants have strong lines, with distinctive, permanent shapes that are often evergreen. On their own they can act as an exclamation mark in the middle of a border or a focal point. However, they lose their emphasis when too many are used together, so it's essential to practise restraint and keep the design simple. The scale of key plants, as with all the structural elements, depends on the scale of the whole garden and the job they need to do; they can be large trees or small shrubs – size isn't everything here, but shape is.

Key plants contribute to the geometry of the garden, highlighting features and leading the eye to focal points within the garden or in the distance outside the garden by framing a view, for example through a port-hole in a hedge.

Astelia chathamica **makes an effective key plant.**

> ### Examples of Good Key Plants
>
> *All trees*   give height
> *Topiary*   all shapes and sizes
> *Hebe*   dome-shaped
> *Dwarf rhododendron*   dome-shaped
> *Pittosporum*   tall dome shape
> *Phormium*   spiky fan shape
> *Astelia*   spiky fan shape
> *Juniper 'Sky Rocket'*   tall column shape
> *Cortaderia*   arching shape

Trees

Trees are an obvious example of structural planting because of their sheer size and bulk. They are an important vertical element in design, contributing by providing height and volume in a way that no other plant can. They can highlight the seasons, with colourful leaves and berries in autumn and winter, and scented flowers in spring or summer. They give shade on a sunny day and provide birds and insects with habitats, food and nesting sites.

Apart from the obvious columnar shape of single trees, there are variations which can draw attention to the horizontal plane. Pleached trees, essentially a row of trees woven together, are carefully pruned to give the effect of a hedge on stilts; they provide structure but still allow a view through the trunks. Consider them to be an investment if you have just the right position for them, they require annual pruning to keep them in shape. Trained fruit trees have been manipulated to grow into shapes that take up very little room and are perfect for small gardens. They have been grafted onto a small root-stock, so they won't grow into a huge tree. Cordons are a popular type: they have a single stem that is restricted by summer pruning and grown at a 45-degree angle. Not only are they productive but their shape also adds structure to the garden.

Double U cordon fruit trees make a decorative partition.

Pyrus salicifolia 'Pendula' makes a statement all by itself.

There is a wide choice, and the decision shouldn't be taken lightly because a mature tree has a great impact on the surroundings for a long time. It may take many years for it to reach full maturity. Take time to consider the best tree for your location and what effect the mature shape will have. A tree with a weeping shape will take up more room than a fastigiated one, whilst a broad-headed tree will take up an average amount of space. The year-round presence of an evergreen tree may seem like a good idea, but it will have a domineering effect and little seasonal change. This may be perfect for some situations, such as highlighting an entrance or screening an ugly view, but such a tree could be oppressive in the wrong setting, such as a small front garden.

Choose the best tree for your garden according to the ultimate dimensions, soil and aspect preferences. The proximity of buildings to trees and more importantly their roots should also be taken into consideration.

Most of us have small gardens, so there is great demand for small ornamental trees, which are not only beautiful but useful.

Small Ornamental Trees

Arbutus unedo Up to 8m tall, evergreen, cinnamon coloured bark, red fruits

Amelanchier lamarckii Up to 10m tall, white flowers in April, autumn tints

Cornus kousa chinensis Up to 7m tall, attractive white bracts in June

Sorbus 'Joseph Rock' Up to 10m high, white flowers in June, amber yellow fruit in autumn

Styrax japonica 8m high, white flowers in June

(Note: The given heights are a guide only; growth may depend on other factors unique to each garden, such as soil type and aspect.)

Hedges

Hedges play an important structural role and can be thought of as the green walls of a garden – defining areas, dividing the space into garden rooms or enclosures that are sheltered places to sit in, perhaps with a choice view of an interesting part of the garden. A solid evergreen hedge provides a complete screen compartmentalizing areas of the garden, whilst a deciduous or semi-deciduous one allows some visibility through to what lies beyond.

Hedges control wind-speed in an exposed garden, filtering the wind to prevent turbulence on the other side of the hedge. Where soil stabilization is a problem they can be used as a remedy to keep soil in place on a bank. They provide structure in a similar way as hard landscaping such as walls, but have a softer, more textural appearance than brickwork and are much less expensive, though they require more maintenance. If the budget is limited and you're patient, choose small bare-rooted hedging plants that are available in the autumn, and wait for them to grow.

The type of plant you use will reinforce the style of the garden. For instance yew can be clipped to a neat crisp shape; it portrays quality, so in a formal, stately home setting you're more likely to see a clipped yew hedge rather than privet. Clipped hedges take up less room than informal billowy ones and can be more

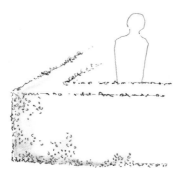

Hedges define and enclose areas in a garden.

suitable for confined areas, such as near a path. The larger leaved varieties, such as hornbeam, can have a more informal shape and a less solid appearance, especially in winter.

Hedges that are too tall to be seen over, on either side of a path, propel you onwards; after all, there's no reason to pause. However the sense of anticipation should be rewarded when you get to the end of the route – something unexpected and different from the previous area of the garden, perhaps a lovely view, a piece of sculpture or interesting planting.

A lower hedge doesn't block your view completely, but can still create a feeling of enclosure or a sheltered spot out of the wind, allowing a feeling of privacy. For a seated person a hedge needs only to be 120cm tall to provide some privacy. Managing the space in this way works well in both small and large gardens; it prevents you from seeing the whole garden and its boundaries at once. If you don't know where the boundaries are you won't immediately know the size and shape of the garden. A handsome pair of structural plants either side of an entrance can be used to announce the way through to a different area of the garden. They can be used both aesthetically and practically, to show an area of steps indicating a change in level.

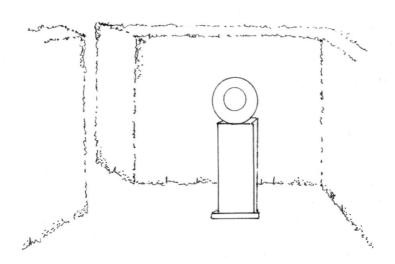

The height of a hedge influences how a garden can be used. Paths enclosed by tall hedges propel the visitor onward. Sculpture provides a focal point

Plants for Hedging

Common name	Botanical Name	Uses
Yew	Taxus baccata	Evergreen, formal clipped shape; topiary
Hornbeam	Carpinus betulis	Semi evergreen, can be clipped as a formal or soft informal shape; larger leaves so not a crisp clipped finish
Privet	Ligustrum Ovalifolium	Fast growing, semi evergreen; can be used formally but needs frequent clipping to keep it in shape
Laurel	Prunus Laurocerasus, Prunus Lusitanica	Has large glossy evergreen leaves, very fast growing
Honeysuckle	Lonicera nitida	Evergreen, fast growing, can be clipped into formal shapes used for topiary
Box	Buxus	Evergreen, formal clipped shape
Fire-thorn	Pyracantha	Evergreen, coloured berries in winter, very thorny, good for boundaries

ORNAMENTAL PLANTS

Ornamental plants are what come to mind for most of us when we think of plants. They provide decoration, colour, foliage, scent, sound and texture. They can produce the glowing autumn colour of Japanese maples or beautifully scented roses, introducing seasonality into the garden so that it looks different through the year. Ornamentals are mostly ephemeral and though they are an essential part of the garden, they should be balanced with structural plants.

With a clear understanding of the structure of the garden, from either plants or hard landscaping, and a plan of how that will work, you can start thinking about the ornamental plants that you want to include. These plants provide dynamism and variety in your planting so that the view changes through the year and you become more aware of seasons.

Plan interesting highlights in the garden such as colour and perfume in winter. Scent is often underused in the garden, but it's an important element adding atmosphere and lifting the spirit in winter with reliable plants such as daphne. The welcome arrival of spring bulbs shows us that winter is coming to an end, and with clever planning when the bulbs die back

An ornamental border including pink cosmos and agapanthus.

there is something exciting to take their place, and so on throughout the year. Remember that if you are away for long periods, you won't want the garden to peak at that time, or have ripe fruit ready when nobody is there to pick it.

Perfume

Making use of our senses adds another dimension that is often overlooked. Scent is very evocative and can release powerful memories of a different time and place. Our senses and appetites are both affected by scent; brush against a rosemary bush and you immediately think of roast lamb. Whilst most scents are pleasant, others such as the curry plant (*Helychrisum angustifoleum*), can be over-powering and unpleasant to some.

Perfume isn't liberally distributed through the plant kingdom. Flowers with brighter colours don't need perfume to attract pollinators, so it's often pale coloured flowers, or plants with small insignificant flowers in winter that rely on perfume. The short days of winter can be improved by the heady perfume of shrubs such as *Sarcococca* (winter box) or *Lonicera purpusii* (winter flowering honeysuckle). Plant them near your main entrance so that they can be enjoyed on a daily basis. Remember that you have to also take into account the aspect of the proposed location, though *Sarcococca* will obligingly grow in light and part-shade. (*See* also Chapter 3.)

Colour

Colour is a valuable part of a garden, affecting our senses and moods; but it's also transient and can't be completely relied on as a main theme. The structural design principles discussed above should be the foundation of the garden, with colour used to enhance it. (Colour is such a large topic that it has its own chapter, *see* Chapter 4.)

Colour plays an important role in plant design.

Lawn

When you think of grass it doesn't immediately spring to mind as being a plant. Nevertheless it is a plant, and like any other requires some thought about where and how it will be used. Whilst it may be both practical and desirable not to have a lawn in a small shady garden, grass is a vital part of many gardens. It can be the 'floor' to the garden room, a restful green backdrop for plants and buildings and of course somewhere for children to play.

Whilst grass has many favourable attributes, it can be very time-consuming to maintain, especially if you want a perfect lawn. Grass needs cutting once a week for much of the year – it hardly stops growing anymore in winter in parts of the UK – whereas a well planned, planted border needs much less attention. A lawn can consume a lot of chemicals in an attempt to eradicate weeds, and take up valuable time coaxing grass to grow in difficult areas such as under trees; like any plant in the garden, there are some areas where grass will not grow successfully.

When designing the garden lay-out beware of putting a lawn in the space that is left over after the borders have been planned. Or conversely, of shaping the borders with what's left over in the garden when the lawn has been planned and marked out. All the components of the garden – borders, lawn, paths and patios – should be in proportion with each other and not merely made of negative space.

Climbing Plants

When the planting is being planned, there will probably be a part of the garden that needs to be screened, either because it's an area that's unattractive, or a part of the garden where a degree of privacy is required from neighbouring houses, or simply a secluded area to enjoy some peace and quiet. Climbing plants are perfect for this, and provide the opportunity to introduce a wider range of plants into the garden. They can scramble over trellis, a blank fence or wall or up into a tree.

Climbing plants can introduce colour, scent, shape and texture into vertical planting: think of the heady perfume of roses and honeysuckle in summer, or the fiery tints and texture of vines in autumn. They can be combined to extend the seasonal interest: a classic combination is a spring-flowering clematis followed by a rose flowering in early summer.

They are particularly useful in small gardens where there isn't much space for plants. Make sure that the conditions are right for the plant and that its

Climbing Plants			
Climbing Plant	*Flowers*	*Position*	*Height*
Actinidia kolomikta	small white, June	sunny SW aspect	5–6m
Akebia quinata (chocolate vine)	maroon scented, March/April	sun/shade, any aspect	6–8m
Berberidopsis corallina	evergreen with crimson, July–Sept	shady S,W aspect	5–7m
Billardiera longiflora	evergreen with green flowers/blue berries, July/Sept	Sun S aspect	2–3m
Hedera (ivy, many varieties)	good for birds and insects	sun or shade	2–3m
Jasminum officinale	scented white, June/Sept	sun S,W, E,	5–6m
Lonicera x americana	fragrant pink-creamy late summer	any aspect, but shy to flower in deep shade	6–7m

ultimate size won't be a problem. On a practical note, remember that structures will be difficult to paint or stain if climbers are grown directly onto them. Better to attach them to trellis or strong wires that can be temporarily detached whilst painting takes place.

Light and Shadows

One of the joys of gardens is that they change constantly. Plants grow, develop, flower, then produce fruit, berries and seeds, and during the summer the garden changes almost on a daily basis. Natural light and shadow is a subtle aspect of planting that can easily be overlooked. Very bright sunshine can appear to bleach softer shades of plants of their colour, whilst the evening sun can be used to advantage, back-lighting plants in summer and making them glow. If bamboo is planted in front of a west-facing wall the shadows will dance across the wall in the evening sun.

It pays to get to know how light and shade affects your garden at different times of the year, so that you can use this to best effect when selecting plants. Artificial light can be used to create shadows in similar ways, as well as its practical application of emphasizing paths, steps and entrances.

Natural light creates shadows to great effect.

SELECTING AND POSITIONING THE PLANTS

Selecting the plants, existing plants, working with shapes, finishing the plan, and making a shopping list

In planting design an understanding of how plants grow, their life cycles and how they're affected by their habitats is immensely useful information. It will help to give you more confidence about the decisions to be made at this stage. The great advantage is that plants really do want to grow and they just need to be given the right conditions.

Plant colonies establish themselves in almost every part of the world, except perhaps ones that have been spoiled by man. A bare patch of ground will soon have plants growing on it, and if the area is ignored and left to grow, these plant colonies will adapt and grow as the conditions change. Small plants grow first, to be joined by other plants that may grow bigger and create shade. This causes some of the original plants, which may need more light to grow, to die out.

The plant group will develop over time as birds and wind bring plant seeds to the site and a wider range of plants begins to grow. Each plant competes for the light and resources that are available locally. They rely on their ability to adapt to the surrounding conditions, and only those most suited to the location will survive. This is why some plants thrive with little help from us, and ideally these are the types of plants that we want to select for our gardens.

OPPOSITE PAGE: **Planting design is about so much more than just putting a few plants in the ground.**

SELECTING THE PLANTS

Which Plants will Prosper?

Gardening with nature rather than against it is a key factor in choosing the right plant. Some locations where plants grow in the wild may be similar to the conditions in our own garden, and we can use this information to help us to choose appropriate plants. A seaside location can be very dry and has little shelter from wind; these exposed conditions can be similar to a roof garden or an exposed garden with poor dry soil. Most plants with silver leaves, narrow rolled leaves or tough leaves will do well in these conditions; silver

Many ferns are very hardy, reliable and easy to grow.

leaves have tiny hairs that protect and trap moisture, whilst narrow leaves have a smaller surface area to lose moisture from.

Plant names can reveal where plants will grow; part of their name may describe their habitat or location: for example *palustris* (meaning of swamps and marshes) as in *Caltha palustris* (marsh marigold), or *sylvatica* (of the woods) in *Fagus sylvatica* (beech).

There are many different terms used in garden reference books and plant labels which can be confusing. Fully hardy, half hardy, or frost tender refer to a plant's ability to cope with cold temperatures. It is safe to say that plants growing in their native habitat will be fully hardy, having adapted perfectly to the conditions in that region. If you take a plant away from its native region where the climate is hotter or colder, we need some form of reference to know whether it will survive.

Evergreen plants are those which stay green through the year, and deciduous plants lose all their leaves in winter and grow new ones in spring. Semi-evergreen plants are those which will only lose their leaves depending on how cold it gets. In a mild winter or region they may be evergreen; in a very cold winter or region they could lose most of their leaves. What determines this is where the plant originates from and the climate it has adapted to.

This is not an exact science and the references used can be misleading or difficult to relate to as temperatures can vary across a county, never mind a continent. In some regions of the UK for example the soil will freeze to a few inches below the surface, while in other milder regions the soil will not freeze at all. This has a big impact on the types of plants which can reliably be grown in the ground depending on where you live. Cities with micro climates in mild regions have many tender plants such as banana and abutilon growing reliably in the ground all year. Just a few miles outside the city, however, they would need to be grown in a conservatory or heated greenhouse.

WHAT ABOUT EXISTING PLANTS?

Few gardens are a blank canvas, and there may be existing plants you need to work into the new planting scheme. Deciding whether to keep existing plants can be as difficult as deciding which new plants to bring in. Even more so if you put them into the garden yourself rather than inheriting them when you moved into the property. Some existing plants can have emotional attachments especially if they were a gift or plants grown from cuttings or seeds. If you are undecided about keeping an existing plant ask yourself a few questions: Is it healthy? Do I like it? Does it fit into the scheme?

If a plant is ailing due to old age, disease or damage and is unlikely to recover the best solution is to dispose of it. If you really like it and it's not easy to find anywhere else try taking cuttings or propagating it before it goes. If you don't like a plant try finding it a new home; the same goes if it just doesn't fit into the new scheme. There may be a friend, neighbour or charity happy to have it. Some plants will not move, either because they are too big, or they do not like root disturbance. These will need to be disposed of. Certain plants are best started from new – particularly hebe, cistus and hardy herbs – as these can get leggy with old wood and are short-lived plants. A new plant will quickly grow and be an asset to the new scheme rather than an eyesore (*see* Chapter 8 for advice about moving plants).

If the plants are staying and not being moved

Paeonia officinalis, whose name indicates its herbal medicinal uses.

to a new position, mark them on the initial plan of the garden and note what they are and how much space they take up. If the plants are staying but being moved, make a note of them, but don't put them onto the plan at this stage; they will be used in the plant list alongside all the new plants you want to use, and as yet you will not know where their final position will be.

FUTURE CLIMATE CHANGES

The debate about climate change will rage on for the foreseeable future and whether it's due to changing weather cycles or the hole in the ozone layer the fact remains that weather patterns are becoming more unpredictable. It looks likely that we can expect more extremes of weather: colder, wetter, hotter or dryer. On islands such as the UK that could all happen in one season if not one day. We can only plan our gardens according to the information available to us and our understanding of that information. All good gardeners will have a basic understanding of physics, botany and geology whether they are aware of it or not, and they know that there will always be next year and the year after to try again.

So how do you plan for the unknown? A few years ago we were told to use drought-tolerant plants in our gardens because the climate would become drier; then parts of the UK had one of wettest summers on record. Next we were told winters will be warmer. Again areas of the UK had the coldest winter for twenty years which meant those who used tender, drought-tolerant plants in their gardens had dead plants to replace.

If you talk to an experienced gardener they will tell you about difficult and unpredictable seasons, about plants they lost but also about plants that fruited for the first time in twenty years. We can all have a willingness to learn, but knowledge backed up by experience is priceless and takes time to acquire. It is also the key to dealing with unpredictable climates and seasons. As a rule winters in the UK tend to be wet and cold; this doesn't suit most Mediterranean plants which

For reliability grow cultivars of native plants such as the holly *Ilex* **'Golden King'.**

can only cope with the cold providing their roots are dry. An olive tree for example can survive frost providing it's not sitting in wet soil. Some plants are only frost or drought tolerant once they are established, so timing the planting to allow them to develop their root system is important (*see* Chapter 8).

Using tough, adaptable plants for the majority of the structure in a garden will help protect the scheme against a changeable and unpredictable climate. Think about using native plants instead of exotic immigrants, or plants which have been cultivated from natives such as box, roses, berberis or cotoneaster. These plants have huge merit and a vast choice of cultivars. When choosing plants which are native to another continent choose those which have adapted to a similar geology and climate, rather than taking a tropical rain forest plant to live in the cold Yorkshire moors or an oak tree to live in the desert.

If the majority of the structure is made up of tough, durable plants this will allow you to use some less reliable ornamental plants in the scheme. Having just a few plants which need cosseting or even replacing if they fail, rather than a whole garden, will be less demanding on your time and budget.

How Quickly Will Plants Grow in your Garden

All plants have their own time scale as to how quickly they grow. We can usually gauge what this will be by the type of plant it is and where it originates from. Plants that have adapted to fertile sheltered conditions in a warm climate will grow quicker, producing softer stems and larger leaves. Plants from barren, harsh landscapes will grow slower, producing harder stems and smaller leaves which are more able to cope with difficult conditions. Aquatic and bog plants are notorious for fast growth because they have a plentiful supply of water and nutrients; they also die back in winter with their roots protected under water, which means they can afford fast growing stems and leaves in the growing season.

Because they die back each year, herbaceous perennials, bulbs and annuals have only a short time to produce flowering stems. They grow quickly in the early part of the year, putting on a lot of growth compared to an evergreen shrub. Deciduous shrubs will often grow at a faster rate than evergreens, producing soft new stems in spring, which will then harden as they age. The term soft or hard wood applies to the stems a plant produces through the year. Soft wood is the young current year's stems,

Plants with large, soft leaves tend to grow more quickly than those with small tough leaves.

and hard wood is found on stems which are more than one year old.

Caution should also be heeded if you choose a large fast growing plant because you want it to do the job quickly. It may well screen the oil tank or unsightly shed in one season, but it will not stop there! It may continue to rampage around the whole garden and your neighbour's, swamping any other plants en route. It will need cutting back regularly which will be hard work, resulting in the plant not flowering or losing its natural shape. A little patience brings great rewards, so choose a plant which is the right size for the space and it will then be well behaved and less work. In the meantime grow some climbing annuals.

A COLLECTION OR A PLANNED SCHEME?

No gardener can resist trying to increase their collection of plants. It's what gardening is all about, collecting plants and growing them. If you see a plant or packet of seeds you have never grown before it can be difficult to say no. But ask yourself, do you want it just because you don't have that particular variety, or because it will fit into the planting scheme in your garden? It's a constant dilemma for anyone who loves growing plants, no matter how much space they have. There will always be something to covet and desire, which is why some people end up with national collections and breeding new varieties. But how can you be both an obsessed collector and a designer?

The range of plants available is vast, but to make planting design easier we need to limit this choice. The style, soil conditions and availability will all help do this, but ultimately you have to stop thinking of the plants in your garden as a collection of individuals. Instead look at them as components of a whole scheme. Rather than have one of everything, try to limit the number of different types of plants used in a garden. This doesn't mean you have to curb your passion – quite the opposite, because designing with plants gives the 'collection' a focus and you a justification for your choices.

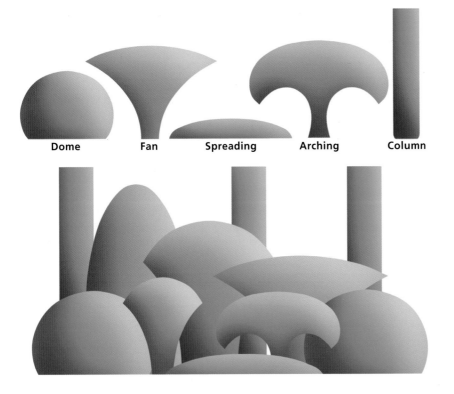

For simplicity when designing use just five different shape categories.

Dome Fan Spreading Arching Column

A combination of all different shapes is confusing and chaotic.

Examples of plant shapes	
Dome	clipped box ball, *Hebe* 'Great Orme', *Viburnum plicatum* 'Mariesii', *Sedum* 'Autumn Joy'
Fan	*Mahonia* x *media* 'Charity', *Euphorbia characias*, *Phormium*, many ferns
Spreading	*Ajuga repens*, *Geranium sanguinium*, *Lamium*, *Epimedium*, *Cotoneaster Horizontalis*
Arching	buddleia, weeping willow, *Spiraea nipponica* 'Snow Mound', *Hemerocallis*
Column	bamboo, *Juniper communis*, *Eucryphia*, *Lysimachia punctata*, foxgloves

WORKING WITH SHAPES

First we look at plant shapes. As plants grow they create a three-dimensional shape which may change as they mature, but essentially they can all be put into a shape category for design purposes. Shrubs and trees tend to have a specific shape from the start, but other plants such as herbaceous perennials change as they grow, so use the shape the plant creates for the longest season.

When looking at the diversity of plants and their different shapes it's difficult to imagine how they can all fit into just five simple categories, but it's a good starting point. Once the principle is understood, the shapes can be adapted to accommodate most plants. For example, many fan-shaped plants are also spiky, such as phormium and cordyline. Clipped box balls may be rounder than a hebe, and bamboo may look more like a tall arching shape than a column. Ultimately the goal is to maintain simplicity by keeping the number of different shapes seen together at the same time to a minimum.

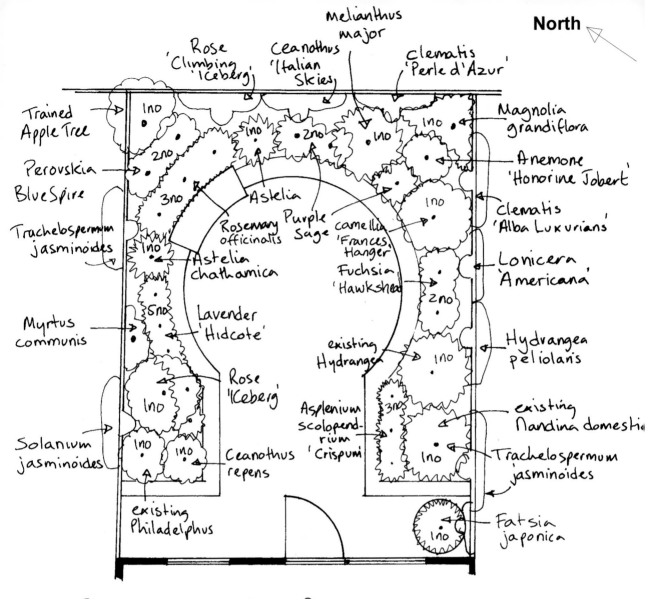

The following labels appear on the planting plan:

- Rose 'Climbing 'Iceberg'
- Ceanothus 'Italian Skies'
- Melianthus major
- Clematis 'Perle d'Azur'
- Trained Apple Tree
- Perovskia Blue Spire
- Trachelospermum jasminoïdes
- Myrtus communis
- Solanum jasminoïdes
- Magnolia grandiflora
- Anemone 'Honorine Jobert'
- Clematis 'Alba Luxurians'
- Lonicera 'Americana'
- Hydrangea petiolaris
- existing Nandina domestica
- Trachelospermum jasminoïdes
- Fatsia japonica
- Astelia
- Rosemary officinalis
- Purple Sage
- Camellia 'Frances Hanger'
- Fuchsia 'Hawkshead'
- Astelia chathamica
- Lavender 'Hidcote'
- Rose 'Iceberg'
- existing Hydrangea
- Asplenium scolopendrium 'Crispum'
- Ceanothus repens
- existing Philadelphus

Planting plan scale 1:50

An example of a professional planting scheme.

Creating a good planting design involves many different considerations and choices. Making some sort of plan helps to organize and make sense of all the information. The rest of this chapter will guide you step by step through the stages of our sample design, applying the information given previously. This formula can be applied to any style of planting and any types of plants, whether it is trees, meadows, formal gardens or prairie planting.

By limiting the number of different shapes used together in a scheme you will create harmony rather than chaos. The plant shapes described here may appear restricting and not very realistic at first, but it's a useful formula that works. There will, of course, be plants that defy being categorized; or the existing climate and conditions may mean plant growth is unpredictable. But that's all the more reason for limiting the shapes in the first place. Once you are confident about putting plant shapes together, you can then look at combining leaf shapes and ultimately flower shapes.

Use Your Garden Centre to Experiment

A good way to try out some design ideas is at a garden centre or nursery, using plants in their pots.

When considering shapes, choose a few plants with strong distinctive shapes, preferably representing the shapes mentioned here. First choose one shape, then add another and see how they look. Then add another shape and see how that works. Keep adding shapes and trying different combinations to get a feel for what works and what doesn't.

When looking at a possible colour scheme this is also a good way to see if it will work in reality.

Experiment at a garden centre by putting different shaped plants together.

The simplest schemes use just one shape, in this case domes.

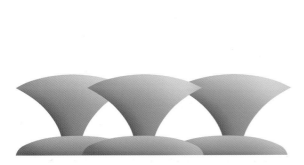

A combination of two different shapes is easy to work with; here are spreading and fan shapes.

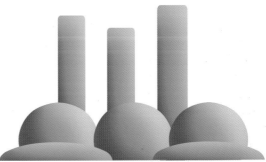

Use a maximum of just three different shapes together, such as spreading, domes and columns.

4.5 metres

1.5 metres

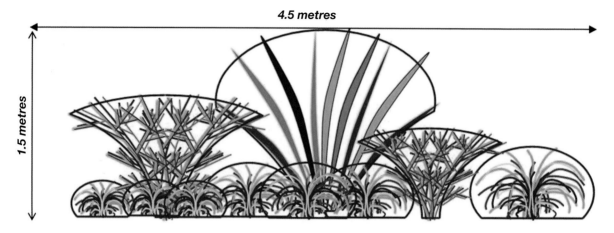

Combinations of different shapes and sizes.

Rather than using all these shapes together in one space and creating chaos and confusion, use just two or three shapes. Also, this will ensure the qualities of the individual plants can be appreciated better and the scheme will have simplicity and harmony.

Using the rule of no more than three distinct shapes together in one space will make it much easier to create a successful planting combination. This can be applied to any type of planting whether it's a mixed border, trees, containers or even plants in a pond. If the plant shapes are simple and compliment each other everything else will fall into place. But if the shapes are too complicated, then it will be frustratingly difficult to bring all the other elements of colour, texture, leaves and flowers together successfully. Each area or border in the garden can have its own different shape combination, but repeating some of the

stronger shapes throughout will create unity and tie the whole design together.

Of course, not all the plants will be the same size, so next you need to think about how tall the plants need to be to do the job. They may be 10m trees or no more than 10cm plants depending on their role and the space they need to fill. You can make a quick sketch showing the different heights and shapes to get a sense of what the scheme will look like. For example, you might have tall domes and low flat domes with tall narrow fans. Or you may have low spreading shapes with big spiky fans.

As discussed in Chapter 5, trees are a huge asset for many reasons and even the smallest space can usually accommodate a tree, it's all a question of scale. A tree can inject a valuable sense of style, place, purpose, even drama in a garden. Designing with them is

Trees come in many wonderful shapes, but the same rules of simplicity and restraint apply.

not difficult if you follow the same formula, keeping the number of different shapes used together to a minimum. Remember, is it just a collection of trees or a planting design?

Designing with plant, leaf and flower shapes all together can get complicated, so it is recommended that you prioritize the plant shape first. Once you are more confident, the next stage is designing with leaves and putting different shapes together to compliment or contrast with each other. The variety of different leaf shapes is vast and the key to designing

with them is, again, limiting the number of strong shapes used together.

Even more of a challenge is then adding flower shapes, but it can be done, especially if you start with one single plant shape. For example spiky fans with sword-shaped leaves, trumpet flowers and feathery foliage could simply be phormium, hemerocallis and fennel. When using shape in planting design the key points to remember are: keep it simple, restrict the amount of different shapes used together and if in doubt, put like with like.

A variety of different leaf shapes.

A variety of different flower shapes.

A variety of different textures found in plant material.

TEXTURE

All plant material will have some kind of texture to it, whether it's rough bark or soft fluffy seedheads. This can be used to add yet another element to the planting, especially when combining contrasting textures together in a scheme. Grey-leaved plants tend to have a soft texture like velvet due to the tiny hairs covering the leaves. Some leaves are very glossy and some are matt and dull. Even if you don't handle the plants, the texture will affect the appearance due the way light is reflected or absorbed. Experiment at home or at the garden centre, putting contrasting textures together and see how they look.

MAKING THE FINAL PLAN

At this stage you are now ready to take all the information you have collated and use it to make a final planting plan. To demonstrate this, the sample brief for a border in Chapter 4 will be taken to the next stage, selecting plants for the final plan and creating a shopping list showing the names of the plants, how many you need and what size pots they should be in. You will also be able see where the filler plants are used to finish the scheme off.

Here is a summary of all the information you need to complete a planting plan. Note that this list includes a number of additions to the original brief, such as the plant and leaf shapes, the plant categories and the heights of the plants that will be needed for this border.

The brief: what you would like to achieve in the garden

The plan and garden analysis: a scaled drawing with notes about the conditions, existing plants, etc

Style of planting: a theme or vision for the whole garden

The colour schemes: combinations which will create the character and seasons

Role of the planting: what job the structural and ornamental plants need to do

Plant and leaf shapes: needed to achieve the three-dimensional element

Plant categories: the types of plants applicable to the scheme (*see* Appendix)

Heights: how high the plants need to be in relation to the rest of the garden

---

Planting Criteria and Requirements for the Sample Border

The Brief

The soil in the garden is a well drained sandy loam with a neutral pH and the border is sheltered from the wind and sunny for most of the day. The position of the border is next to the kitchen door and can be seen from inside the house so needs to look good all year. The planting needs to include some herbs for cooking, and the style should be naturalistic with some strong dramatic shapes. The colour scheme should be pretty but sophisticated using soft greys and greens with yellow, purple and white flowers, but maybe some dark leaves for a bit of drama.

Planting Criteria	Requirements
Position of planting space in garden	Border outside kitchen door
Function of space	Supply some herbs for the garden and provide view from kitchen window
Style of garden/space	Naturalistic style with mixed flowering plants but some dramatic shapes
Seasons of interest	All year
Aspect and conditions	Sunny with well-drained neutral soil
Fragrance	Summer and autumn
Budget	Medium/low
Maintenance levels	Medium/low
Leaf colour x 3 max	Silver grey, green and purple/brown
Stem & bark colour x 3 max	Grey, silver, purple/brown
Flower colour x 3 max	White, yellow and purple
Plant shapes x 3 max	Domes, narrow fans and spiky fans
Leaf shapes x 3 max	Swords, linear and oval
Heights min and max	Min 10cm, max 1.5m
Plant categories	Key plants, structural evergreens, ornamental shrubs and perennials, bulbs and annuals

If it makes it easier the criteria can be put into a table, but this format can be used for any type of planting design.

Making the Final Selection

To proceed with our sample border, here is the list of plants that we have initially chosen for this scheme.

Even though all these plants fit the criteria of the brief, there are still too many and the list needs to be reduced. First take out those that will not be needed in this border, such as trees and climbers. Then discard any that will be too big, in this case any plants over 1.5m high.

Now decide on which shapes you would like to use – here we have decided to use domes, fans and spiky fans. Only the plants that fit these criteria will remain, and they have been highlighted on the table.

Season	Trees	Climbing and wall shrubs	Evergreen shrubs	Deciduous shrubs	Evergreen perennials, ferns and grasses	Deciduous perennials, ferns and grasses	Annuals or bi-annuals	Bulbs
Spring	Amelanchier lamarckii	Clematis alpina Ceanothus 'Italian Skies' Clematis montana grandiflora	Myrtus communis (dome) Magnolia stellata (dome) Rosemarinus officinalis (dome)	Deutzia gracilis (dome) Spirea 'Arguta' (arching) Syringa vulgaris 'Charles Joly' (arching) Elaeagnus quicksilver (arching)	Epimedium x youngianum 'Niveum' (spreading)	Iris 'Sable' (spiky fan) Iris pallida 'Variegata' (spiky fan) Pulmonaria officinalis 'Sissinghurst White' (spreading)	Cerinthe major (arching) Aquilegia alpina (column)	Tulip 'Spring Green' (spiky fan) Daffodil Tete a Tete (spiky fan)
Summer	Cornus kousa 'China Girl'	Rose climbing 'Iceberg' Clematis 'Alba Luxurians' Clematis 'Perle d'Azur' Trachelospermum jasminoides	Lavender 'Hidcote' (dome) Ceanothus 'Autumn Blue' (fan) Cistus x corbariensis (dome) Salvia officinalis (dome) Convolvulus cneorum (dome)	Philadelphus coronarius 'Variegatus' (arching) Rose 'Glamis Castle' (fan) Rose 'Graham Thomas' (fan) White Hibiscus (fan)	Stachys byzantina 'Big Ears' (spreading) Libertia grandiflora (spiky fan)	Pennisetum orientale (fan) Centaurea montana (dome) Dianthus 'Mrs Sinkins' (dome) Eryngium alpinum (fan) Geranium himalaynse (dome) Hemerocallis citrinella (spiky fan) Lychnis coronaria 'Alba' (fan)	Convolvulus sabatius (dome)	Lilium regale (column)
Autumn		Passiflora caerulea 'Constance Elliot' Parthenocissus henryana	Hebe 'Autumn Glory' (dome) Buddleja davidii 'Empire Blue' (fan)	Perovskia 'Blue Spire' (fan)	Melianthus major (arching) Fuchsia 'Hawkshead' (arching)	Anemone x hybrida 'Honorine Jobert' (tall dome) Verbena bonariensis (column)	Nicotiana sylvertris (arching)	Dahlia 'White Ballet' (fan)
Winter		Chaenomeles speciosa 'Nevalis' Garrya elliptica	Box balls Sarcoccoca humilis (dome)		Astelia chathamica (spiky fan)			Snowdrops (spiky fan)
All year	Weeping Pear	Hedera helix 'Eva'	Euonymus fortunei 'Silver Queen' (dome) Choisya 'Aztec Pearl' (dome) Hebe albicans (dome) Osmanthus x burkwoodii (tall dome) Pittosporum 'Garnettii' (tall dome)		Cortaderia selloana 'Pumilla' (arching) Cotoneaster franchettii (arching) Astelia chathamica (spiky fan) Helleborus argutifolius (arching)			

The table on page 71 has now been refined using only those plants (highlighted) that are suitable for this border.

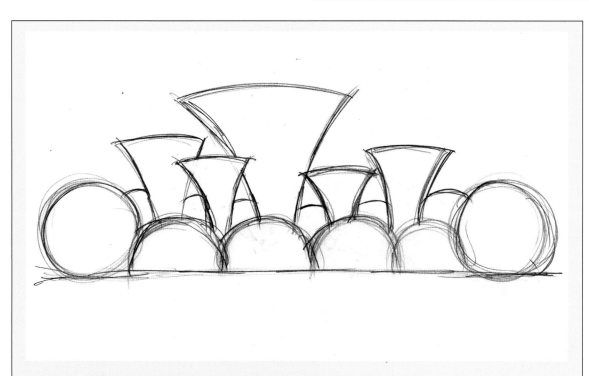

(1) Make a sketch to check that the shapes and heights work together.

(2) Draw your survey or plan with any existing plants marked on it, preferably to a scale of 1:50 or 2cm:1m.

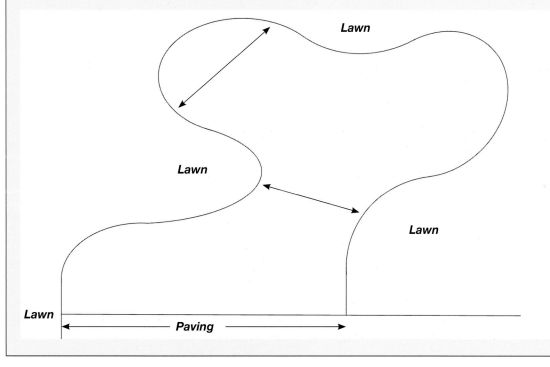

Position Plants on the Sample Plan

When you have a reduced list of plants and have a clear idea of what each plant will bring to the scheme you can start to position them on the sample plan.

First the planting spaces need to be defined. This means allocating spaces for the different plant categories such as key plants, structural and ornamental plants. You will only be using a few different categories in each border; other areas of the garden will require different categories such as trees and climbers, and some may have only groundcover plants, depending on the role of the plants and the overall design of the garden.

You now need to allocate spaces for the other categories of plants. A space may accommodate one large plant or several smaller plants which will grow together to make a drift or clump. Don't make the spaces too small or the scheme will look bitty. You do not need to decide yet what the plants will be, but you can make a note of what height and colour they will be.

Those plants that will be fillers, such as seasonal bulbs and annuals, will not be allocated a space on the plan because they will grow through and between the permanent planting. Simply make a note of where you would like them to be, or you can even wait until the plants are in the ground.

Only at this stage can you begin to get a realistic idea of how the plant partnerships will work together. The number of plants actually used may seem very small, but this will benefit the simplicity and success of the scheme in the long term. There will be plants still on the list which haven't been used. Don't be tempted to squeeze them in though, because next you need to work out how many plants will fit into each space. It may be far fewer than you think. Keep your original list handy because you can use it to choose alternatives and for schemes in other parts of the garden.

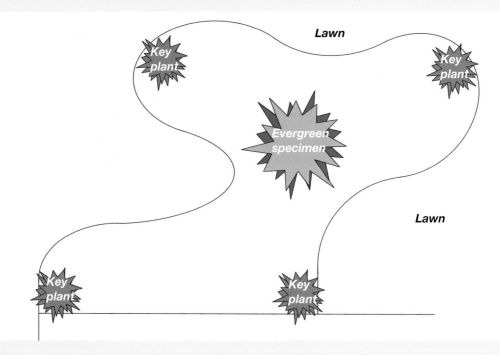

(3) Position the key plants, making sure they relate to the overall design, highlighting the architecture of the garden (you may know at this stage what these will be).

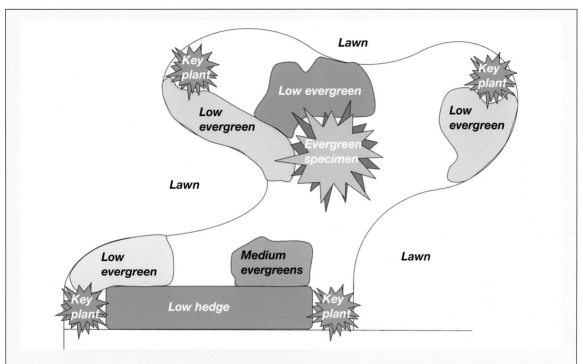

(4) Allocate space for the other structure plants, making a note of whether they need to be low, medium or high and the colour, leaving enough space for the ornamentals.

(5) Now fill the spaces between with the ornamentals, again noting their height and colours.

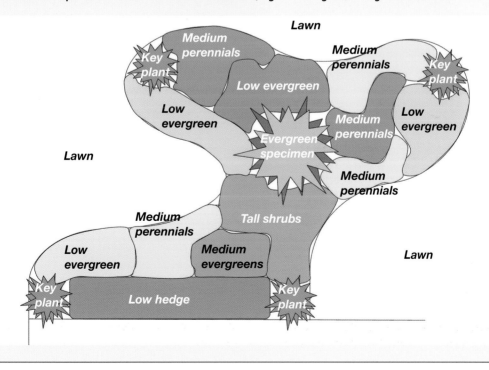

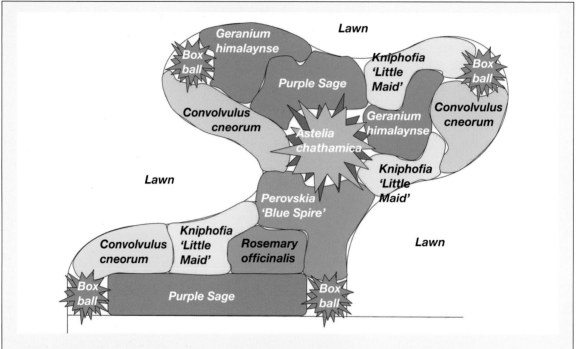

Using the list of plants, decide which will fit the design and write them on the plan.

Plant Spacing

Knowing how much space plants need to grow is not an exact science. Reference books and plant labels can be contradictory or confusing. Growing conditions and aftercare will affect a plant's performance enormously. The best you can do is estimate how much space you think a plant might need, based on research and if possible, your own experience. However, you will need to accept that the plant may grow more or less than expected and adjustments will need to be made.

How Much Space to Allow for a Plant?

This is a very simple guide for working out how much space to give each type of plant on the ground. The dot in the centre of the circle represents the centre of the plant.

Height	Type of Plant
30cm	very small perennials, rock plants and biennials
45cm	small perennials and biennials
30–60cm	hedging plants
60cm	small evergreen and deciduous shrubs and medium sized perennials
1m	medium and large evergreen shrubs, medium deciduous shrubs and large perennials
1.3m	large deciduous shrubs
3m and upwards	small to large trees

[Note: climbing plants and wall shrubs should be spaced between 2–3m apart with 60cm–1m space on the ground]

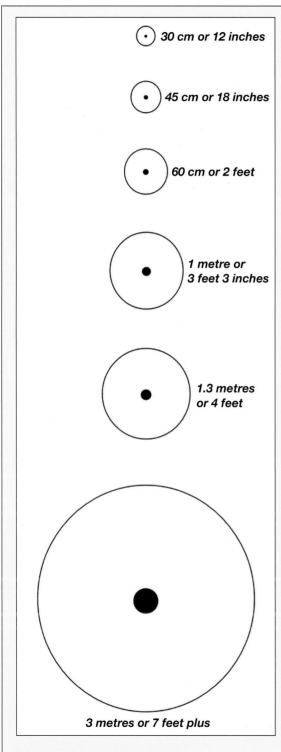

30 cm or 12 inches

45 cm or 18 inches

60 cm or 2 feet

1 metre or
3 feet 3 inches

1.3 metres
or 4 feet

3 metres or 7 feet plus

A spacing formula using circles.

Professional designers will all have their own formulas and guides for spacing plants based on experience, gathered knowledge and common sense. To accommodate different growing conditions, they may vary their formula slightly to suit individual projects. Ultimately having a simple spacing guide to follow is a good place to start.

Circles are often used to represent a plant's growing space because most plants will grow symmetrically and fill a circular space on the ground. Of course there are exceptions to this. Plants that have been damaged or don't have sufficient light can make odd shapes, but these are due to external circumstances which can or cannot be controlled. Also groundcover plants will spread where they can, while climbing plants will grow where there is support. At this stage we are looking at the space we expect them to take up on the ground, which most plants with sufficient light and good growing conditions can be expected to achieve.

Purple sage is an excellent border plant which can also be used in the kitchen.

Putting the Plants on the Sample Plan

You now need to draw the plant spaces on the plan; use a circle template if you like.

You can now see how many plants are required to fill each allocated space. Try to leave as little empty space around the plants as possible, but don't overlap the circles too much or there will not be enough room for the plants to grow. Now you can also see where the fillers will be used, in the spaces between the circles.

CREATING A SHOPPING LIST

You now have a list of plants and the quantities you need to fill the border.

Plants

- 12 *Geranium himalayense*
- 13 *Kniphofia* 'Little Maid'
- 4 box ball
- 8 purple sage
- 10 *Convolvulus cneorum*
- 2 *Rosemary officinalis*
- 1 *Astelia chathamica*
- 5 *Perovskia* 'Blue Spire'

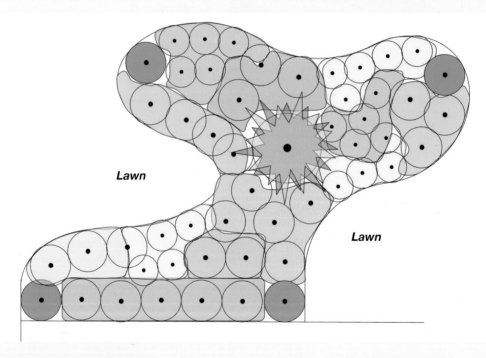

How the circles fit onto the plan.

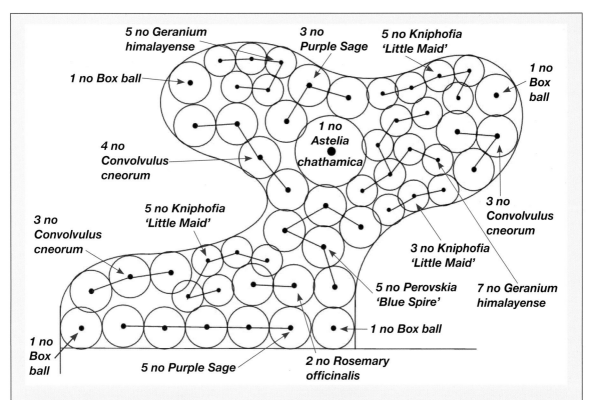

5 no Geranium himalayense

3 no Purple Sage

5 no Kniphofia 'Little Maid'

1 no Box ball

1 no Box ball

1 no Astelia chathamica

4 no Convolvulus cneorum

3 no Convolvulus cneorum

3 no Convolvulus cneorum

5 no Kniphofia 'Little Maid'

3 no Kniphofia 'Little Maid'

7 no Geranium himalayense

5 no Perovskia 'Blue Spire'

1 no Box ball

1 no Box ball

5 no Purple Sage

2 no Rosemary officinalis

How many plants will be needed?

Convolvulus cneorum with purple-flowered *Convolvulus sabatius*.

Fillers (these quantities have been estimated)

Annuals and short-lived perennials:
- 10 *Aquilegia vulgaris*
- 5 *Verbena bonariensis*
- 1 packet of *Cerinthe major* seeds

Bulbs:
- Dwarf daffodils
- Snowdrops
- Alliums

Which Size Plants to Buy?

When buying a new plant you may have difficulty imagining that what you see in the pot will, given time, grow much bigger and take up all the space you have allowed it on the plan, but it will. Buying plants and budgeting is discussed in more detail in Chapter 7, but the size of the new plant you choose will probably depend on how much they cost or what is available. There is a wide range of different sized pots which plants are sold in, ranging from tiny to enormous, and it is useful at this stage to understand how this relates to the plan and the plants you will buy to put into the ground.

Final Plant Shopping List with Pot Sizes Required

Plants:
- 12 *Geranium himalayense* 1lt pot (small pots because the plants grow quickly)
- 13 *Kniphofia* 'Little Maid' 1lt pot
- 4 Box ball 10lt pot (a large pot because box is slow growing and they are important key plants)
- 8 Purple sage 1lt pot
- 10 *Convolvulus cneorum* 1lt pot
- 2 *Rosemary officinalis* 3lt pot (a medium sized pot because rosemary is part of the structure)
- 1 *Astelia chathamica* 10lt pot (a large pot because the astelia is an important key plant)
- 5 *Perovskia* 'Blue Spire' 3lt pot

Fillers (annuals and short lived perennials):
- 10 *Aquilegia vulgaris* 0.5lt pot (small pots because these are only fillers and will grow quickly)
- 5 *Verbena bonariensis* 0.5lt pot

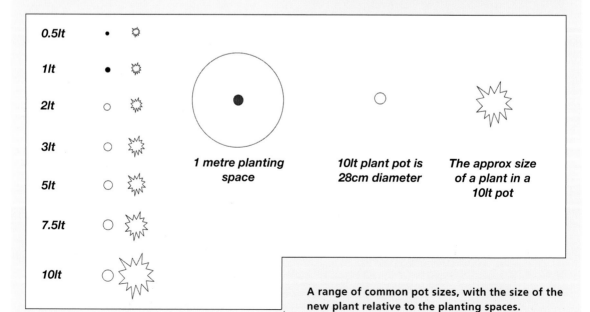

0.5lt		
1lt		
2lt		
3lt		
5lt		
7.5lt		
10lt		

1 metre planting space

10lt plant pot is 28cm diameter

The approx size of a plant in a 10lt pot

A range of common pot sizes, with the size of the new plant relative to the planting spaces.

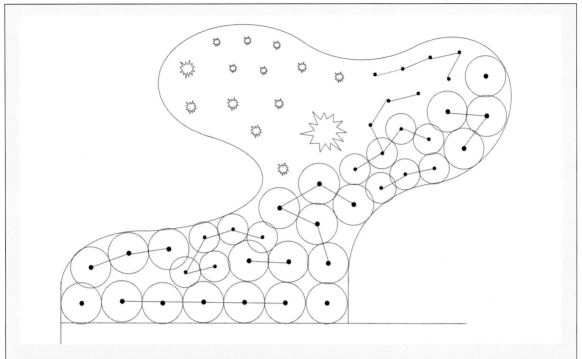

What the plants look like when they are first put in the ground, in relation to the plant spaces they have been given.

A mixed border with soft purple, blue and silver.

From these diagrams you can see that when new plants are first put into the ground, there will be a lot of empty spaces. It will be very tempting to move the plants closer together or add more to fill the gaps – but don't. This will simply result in overplanting, which will be a waste of money, plants, time and energy. These gaps will gradually get smaller as the plants grow and mature; in the meantime you can cover the bare soil with a mulch of bark chips or garden compost to help prevent weeds growing and keep moisture in. Over the next few years you can use any temporary 'fillers' you want to go into these gaps until the all the plants grow together.

The next chapter will discuss how to source, buy, grow or acquire the plants on your list.

TURNING THE PLANT LIST INTO REALITY

Working with existing plants, sourcing plants, choosing alternatives, budgeting, timing your planting

Existing plants can be incorporated into the new scheme.

At this stage the carefully chosen plants are just a list of names on a piece of paper. So where do they come from, how big should they be and how much will they cost? Also, what happens to the existing plants already in the garden? This chapter will help you take a list of plants and turn them into reality with as little waste of time, money and energy as possible.

OPPOSITE PAGE: **At specialist plant nurseries you can get information from the people who grow the plants.**

WORKING WITH EXISTING PLANTS

We have discussed existing plants in terms of how to decide whether they should stay or go, but what do you do with the existing plants that are to be incorporated into the new scheme?

Some trees and shrubs that are to stay in their original positions may need reducing or reshaping, and this should be done before starting to plan, if possible, so you will get a better idea of the space that remains. The same applies if plants are to be removed.

But plants that are to be lifted and moved to a new position will need some thought and more of this is discussed in Chapter 8.

SOURCING PLANTS

Before completing the wish list of plants, it's useful to know whether you will be able to get them or not. Some plants can always be difficult to find; others may be scarce just when you want them. Some may need to be ordered from specialist growers, or you may need to wait for the right time of year, as in the case of bulbs and bare-rooted plants. There are many places to buy plants from, but there are also many opportunities for low cost or even free plants. So where do you start looking? The *RHS Plant Finder* is an excellent resource used by professionals and amateurs. It is available as a book which is published each year, or on the internet, listing which nurseries stock which plants in the UK (*see* Further Information).

Plant Availability

Experienced designers will know which plants are easily available, those which can be unpredictable and those which may need to be searched for. But some years or seasons even common plants can become scarce. This may be due to the commercial growers having difficulty with extreme weather conditions, or they may decide to drop that particular plant from their list. Sometimes seed can be difficult to obtain or cuttings fail. There may even have been a project somewhere that called for a huge number of one particular type of shrub, with few left on the market for sale. If a plant is very new to the market, growers might be reluctant to try it in large numbers in case it fails commercially.

Not all plants are happy to grow in containers. Some such as bamboo will outgrow their pots before they can be sold because they are so vigorous. Many plants can only be grown successfully in gardens from seed and as a result are rarely available in pots,

such as the beautiful *Cerinthe major* and many other annuals or biennials. Bulbs such as snowdrops are best planted 'in the green' after they have flowered rather than from dried bulbs. Roses, hedging and fruit trees are sold 'bare rooted' in the autumn, which is much cheaper than buying them in containers.

Buying from Garden Centres

The most obvious place to start looking for plants might be a retail outlet such as a garden centre. There is a wide range of garden centres; they vary enormously and shouldn't be judged simply on their coffee shop.

A good one will have a wide range of healthy plants which are cared for by knowledgeable and experienced staff. They should give you comprehensive advice about buying and growing the plants and be willing, if possible, to order plants in for you that they don't normally stock. All the plants should be healthy, clearly labelled and priced. They should be in clean, tidy pots with no weeds growing in the compost. There should be no roots growing out the bottom of the pot, as this means it will probably be pot bound. Garden centres should also give a guarantee that if plants fail within a certain amount of time, they will replace them or give you a refund. It's worth checking a garden centre's policy on returns if buying a large order. All this comes at a price, and naturally the plants will cost more at good garden centres because you are getting a quality product and a first class service.

If you have a long list of plants which includes trees, shrubs and herbaceous perennials, even the best garden centre will struggle to supply all the plants in the sizes and quantities you want. They may be able to order many of them in for you, or offer you good alternatives, but there will still be certain plants they cannot get when you need them. Even professional designers can have a few items on the list which are difficult to find. Professional garden designers can use the services of wholesale suppliers who will source plants from growers all over the UK and even Europe. They will collect the plants together and deliver them on an agreed date, either altogether or in stages

Plants like this rose 'Wildeve' can survive being sent in the post.

A good, local garden centre is essential for any serious gardener.

depending on the size of the order. This makes setting out the scheme much easier, as all the plants can be positioned and adjustments made before they go in the ground.

Specialist Nurseries, Mail Order and the Internet

Another place to look for plants is specialist nurseries. These can be very rewarding places to visit, with the best advice possible from the people who grow the plants. A nursery local to you is even better, because the plants will have adapted to the growing conditions and climate in your region. Your garden will be like a home from home for the plants.

For many years nurseries and growers have sold plants by mail order, delivered to your door through the post. It's been tried and tested and works very well, providing you are around to receive the order. The new plants need to be attended to as soon as possible. An extreme example of this was a delivery of bare-root roses that arrived before Christmas from a renowned rose grower. Unfortunately, the recipient was not able to take delivery of the order so they sat in their packaging for nearly two weeks at the post office. Despite this, they survived and are now very healthy plants, but this is not to be recommended.

Most specialist nurseries now have websites and sell plants on line, which is a fantastic way of choosing and buying plants. They ensure that bulbs, fruit bushes and trees which have shorter planting seasons will only be delivered to you when they are ready to go into the ground, even if you place the order months in advance. Early ordering has other advantages, as some popular varieties will be sold out quickly.

Plant Fairs and Flower Shows

There are many excellent flower shows held through the year all around the country, either local or regional. They are very good places for buying plants or finding

Buying plants from flower shows can provide unusual varieties and add excitement and happy memories to your garden.

specialist nurseries to order plants from. You can meet the growers and get valuable advice, information and inspiration for new planting schemes. Many are held by the Royal Horticultural Society and other organizations; others include the Rare Plant Fair and The Plant Hunters' Fair. There are also annual regional shows such as Southport Flower Show and Harrogate Flower Show.

Plant Sales

Gardens open for charity, school fetes and church bazaars are all great places to buy plants with some wonderful bargains. They are usually very reasonably priced and the plants are often fresher than those sold in garden centres. Just watch out for weeds, pests and incorrect labelling, and remember, you may be looking for a bargain, but they are collecting for charity.

Supermarkets and DIY Stores

If a plant is healthy and for sale at a reasonable price, it shouldn't matter where you buy it from, other than ethical and environmental concerns. But that applies to everywhere we shop. Many perfectly good plants are sold in supermarkets and DIY stores; the only disadvantage is their short shelf life. Plants need to be tended and cared for, whereas a packet of nails or a box of cereal does not. But if a plant is on your list, looks fresh and healthy, then pop it in the shopping trolley with the milk. Many retailers will have a bargain shelf with products they wish to clear, and some gardeners see buying plants from here more as a rescue mission than a discerning purchasing choice.

Acquiring from Friends

For generations plants have been given away by friends, families and acquaintances. There is a culture between keen gardeners that if someone admires a plant in your garden you should give them a 'bit'. This 'bit' could be a cutting, some seeds or a clump dug out of the ground and popped into a plastic bag. If you're lucky it's a cutting or seedling that has been potted up and grown into a nice little plant, but it's all part of the philosophy of spreading about something which is good and worthwhile. It is also an insurance policy for the grower. If their plant dies they know where to get another cutting or handful of seed to start again. Whole families, groups of friends and even streets may all have the same plant in their gardens which has been carefully distributed by an obsessive gardening matriarch or patriarch.

Whilst this tradition is to be celebrated and encouraged, it can present a moral issue for someone acquiring plants from a carefully chosen list. Refusing a generous offer of a free plant is a bit like the young new home owner being offered furniture the rest of the family no longer wants. Also, a delicate treasure in one person's garden may turn into a rampaging weed

Cerinthe major **can be easily grown from seed, but is rarely seen in pots for sale.**

in another more fertile and clement setting. The offering may be carrying invasive perennial weeds such as ground elder or bindweed, so keep the pot in quarantine for a while before planting it in the ground to check what else is in there.

Growing your Own: Propagating

Propagating and growing your own plants is probably the most satisfying and rewarding activity any gardener can do. This is not necessarily about saving

money; the paraphernalia available for propagating is endless and costly. But it can also be done on a very modest budget. Of course, if you grow all the plants yourself it would take many years for the garden to reach maturity. This may suit you, but bear in mind that when buying plants already grown at a certain size we are buying time.

The ultimate propagation set-up is the heated green house, cold frame and potting shed, with compost in labelled bins and clean pots and seed trays stacked neatly waiting to be used. For most of us the reality is the kitchen window sill and a few recycled yoghurt pots. Either way, the propagation of plants is very special, and every gardener should at least have a go. If you don't have the time, budget, space or inclination to grow all your own plants, but would like to grow something, choose plants which would otherwise be either difficult to find, very expensive or only available to buy as seeds.

Not all seeds or cuttings need to be grown indoors; many can be grown outside either in the ground or in pots. Some can only be grown outside, because they need cold temperatures to germinate. The fact that pruned stems used as plant supports will often root shows how easy it can be. Plants spend all their lives trying to propagate themselves. Producing seed is the most obvious example, but many will spread themselves freely by sending out stems and branches which root in the ground and produce a whole new plant which can be lifted and replanted (this is called layering).

Managing Overcrowded Perennials

You have probably noticed that herbaceous perennials can become overcrowded if left unattended in the ground for too long, often resulting in few or no flowers and a mass of leaves. They benefit from being lifted, split up and sections replanted. But essentially they have propagated themselves even if they needed the gardener to help them. In the wild such plants would get disturbed by animals digging, and the clumps that got scattered about would then grow and multiply.

Be aware that if you decide to produce plants to sell, many are now protected under copyright, and it is illegal to propagate and sell them commercially without permission from the grower. Plant labels will usually say if a plant is copyright protected, but not always.

Herbaceous perennials can get overcrowded and benefit from being lifted, split up and sections replanted.

The availability of some plants can be unpredictable, such as the tender silk tree *Albizia julibrissin*.

CHOOSING ALTERNATIVES

It seems with almost any list there is at least one plant that you cannot find anywhere, either for sale or to acquire. Or it might be for sale but the sizes on offer are either too big or too small. If the only *Camellia japonica* 'Janet Waterhouse' available to buy is in a huge 25lt pot and costs as much as the total plant budget, you may need to think again. If it is only being offered in a 3lt pot and you want a good sized mature plant, you may need to think about using an alternative. You can of course wait until one becomes available, but this can be frustrating, especially if there are several plants on the list like this.

If you want to keep the integrity of the scheme and not make heavy compromises, choosing alternatives can be tricky. After all, too great a compromise would be a shame since so much thought and consideration has gone into creating the list in the first place. There is as much skill involved in choosing alternatives as in creating the original planting scheme. It is very much part of the whole design process. This is why professional designers will often put 'no substitutes without prior consultation' on their plants lists when submitting them to the suppliers. The good news is that plant species are many and varied, and there will always be a suitable alternative, even if a little lateral thinking is required.

The first place to look for a good alternative is your original list of plants, as there may be something you can use instead of the plant you can't get hold of. Alternatively look at the attributes of your first choice and choose a plant with similar attributes. With a plant like the white flowered *Camellia japonica* 'Janet Waterhouse' this is quite straightforward; there are many other white flowered camellias to choose from. They may have slight variation in their plant shape and size, flowering season and colour, so you still need to check it fits into the scheme. But if the plant you want is not from a large family of cultivars you may then need to look at a different species altogether and decide which attributes from the original choice have the greatest priority. Remember, the alternative choice will need to suit the same conditions, since these will not change.

Let's take an example: *Eucryphia* x *nymansensis* 'Nymansay' is a slow-growing evergreen tree. In five years, depending on its size when it is planted, it

	Plant name	Conditions	Attributes
Original Choice	Eucryphia x *nymansensis* 'Nymansay'	Moist, acid soil and full sun	Height 5m Evergreen Column shape White flowers Season: summer/autumn Plant category: tree Fragrant flowers

Table showing plant name, preferred conditions and attributes.

might reach 5 metres. Potentially it could reach 50 metres, but only after many years. It has a column shape and white flowers in late summer and autumn. It needs acid soil which is moist at its roots, but it likes full sun at its crown.

Consider these attributes and place them in order of priority. Here the most important attribute is the height of the plant; next, that it is evergreen and column shaped. A plant like this would be a strong structural element in the design, so its height, shape and evergreen quality is vital. Next are the flowers. The scheme may or may not have a white in the colour scheme, but maybe the alternative needn't have flowers at all for it to do the job. This also applies to the season. In this example, eucryphia being a tree is a low priority. It takes many years for it to look like a tree rather than a large shrub, so a shrub may also work. Lastly we have fragrance. The fact that eucryphia flowers are fragrant is an added bonus to an already beautiful plant, but fragrance is ephemeral and could be supplied by placing another fragrant plant nearby.

These priorities could change depending on the function of the plant in the whole scheme. If white flowers and fragrance became the highest priority, you may need to consider whether a deciduous shrub or small tree would be more suitable. Making the decision should be based on the role the plant is to perform in the relation to the other plants in the scheme.

So what alternative could we use instead of the eucryphia, assuming that another plant from the same family is not an option? If we take the conditions and the most important attribute, we are looking for evergreen plants which like acid soil and sun. The list may look like this: magnolia, conifer, bamboo, box, camellia, crinodendron, kalmia, pieris, rhododendron.

Then we look at the next priority, which is a column shape, and remove from the list all those which do not fit: box, crinodendron, kalmia, pieris, and rhododendron. These will all make dome-shaped plants. The

Magnolia grandiflora.

	Plant Name	Conditions	Attributes
Original Choice	*Eucryphia* x *nymansensis* 'Nymansay'	Moist, acid soil and full sun	Evergreen Column shape Height: 5m–50m (but slow growing) White flowers Season: Summer/autumn Tree Fragrant
Alternative Choice	*Magnolia grandiflora* 'Little Gem'	Moist, acid soil and full sun	Evergreen Column shaped Height: 4m–6m White flowers Season: summer/autumn Tree Fragrant

Table comparing the original plant with the alternative choice.

box could be trained into a column shape, but that may not be practical at the size needed. This leaves magnolia, camellia, conifer and bamboo.

The next attribute is height, and the camellia may not get tall enough. So we're left with magnolia, conifer and bamboo. Neither the conifer nor the bamboo has flowers, so that leaves magnolia. Some magnolias are deciduous but *Magnolia grandiflora* is evergreen and even flowers in late summer and autumn. *Magnolia grandiflora* 'Little Gem' would be a good choice. It may not get quite as tall as some other varieties, but it has the column shape we want, and its flowers are fragrant.

Nurseries and garden centres will be able to help you with finding alternatives, but remember, you need to emphasize the main attributes you require in order for them to find a suitable alternative. Many plants of the same family can look completely different. *Elaeagnus angustifolia* 'Quick Silver' for example makes a small deciduous tree with narrow, silver grey leaves and sweet smelling flowers in early summer; while *Elaeagnus ebbingii* is a dense evergreen shrub with tiny fragrant flowers in autumn and is good for hedging. The two plants perform completely different roles in a garden, yet *ebbingii* is often offered as an alternative to 'Quick Silver'. Again the *RHS Plant Finder* is an excellent place to look for alternatives.

Elaeagnus ebbingii.

Elaeagnus angustifolia 'Quicksilver'.

BUDGETING

How Much Should you Spend?

The main disadvantage of an instant garden is cost. Bigger plants are far more expensive than smaller ones. But there is also the practical aspect of moving large containers and digging large holes in the ground for them to go into. In addition, large trees and shrubs may take longer to get established than smaller plants.

The alternative to having an instant garden is to use much smaller plants and wait for them to grow. The disadvantage of this is all the bare soil between the plants while you wait for them to grow, which could look unsightly and be a potential nursery for weeds. A compromise is to have a few larger plants with the majority of them being smaller. In the resulting bare earth between, grow temporary fillers such as annuals, biennials and bulbs, which will gradually be pushed out as the garden matures but will not compete or adversely impact on the scheme. Do not be tempted to plant shrubs to fill the gaps, as these will compromise the scheme and you will have simply overplanted.

As with any budget it's a case of prioritising and spending money as economically as possible. Some plants naturally grow much quicker than others. For example a philadelphus can double in size in two years, while a rhododendron may look exactly the same as when it was planted. It makes sense to invest in a larger slow-growing plant and economize on those which grow and mature quickly. It also depends on how critical a plant is to the design and overall structure of a scheme. Buying a very small box ball which is underpinning the whole design and waiting for it to grow can be frustrating and disappointing. Better to save money on the easy, fast-growing plants and invest in a good size specimen that will give you instant impact and enjoyment.

Very large plants are available at specialist nurseries, which will also deliver the plants to your house and advise about planting.

TIMING

How Long Will the Garden Take to Mature?

Designers are often asked, how long will the garden take to mature? The answer is always difficult because there are so many varying factors such as the soil conditions, climate, maintenance, type of plant and so on. As mentioned, budget is one of the main factors which will decide the size of the plants you buy, but if your wish list has mostly slow-growing evergreens, you will either need to wait a long time for them to mature or buy bigger plants. These will inevitably be more expensive because the growers will have had to look after them for longer before selling them on. The faster growing deciduous shrubs and perennials on your list can be bought as smaller plants and therefore they will be cheaper. This is why existing plants can be such an asset in a new scheme, especially if they are already mature. On average, a newly planted garden should be looking fairly mature after five years. After five years some of the planting may need to be reviewed and adjusted slightly depending on how well the plants have grown.

Buying and Planting

Buying and collecting plants for a planting scheme may take a few months or a few days. However long it takes, most of the plants will prefer to go straight into the ground once you get them home, providing the conditions are favourable. Some plants may be happy to sit in a pot for a while before being planted, providing they are cared for, but you need the space to store them and time to look after them. If possible, plan the buying and planting to coincide. (*See* Chapter 8 for information on preparing for planting.)

A well-planned border will be a pleasure for many years.

PREPARING FOR PLANTING

What makes plants grow? Improving the soil, using compost, tools, how to plant, mulching

Peony 'Solange'.

Successful planting design relies on composing together all the aesthetic elements of plants such as shape, form, scale, contrast and colour. But for real long-term garden success there also has to be an understanding of plant ecology: how plants grow, how they are affected by different types of soil and what they need for optimum growth. Having spent

OPPOSITE PAGE: **Topiary box with heuchera and cardoons.**

time and energy planning a planting design, make sure that the essential requirements, such as good soil, are available for plants and that proper planting techniques will be used to get the plants off to a good start.

Quite simply, a plant needs water, food and light to grow. The roots anchor the plant into the soil and stabilize it, reaching deep down to access the water and nutrients that it needs. A well-established, mature plant has an extensive root system resulting

A mixed planting scheme creates colour and structure.

in a large surface area that allows maximum absorption of resources from the surrounding soil. However, a new plant can only take up a restricted amount of water and nutrients, because it has an immature root system and a small number of leaves that limit the level of photosynthesis. The fine root hairs of bare-rooted or larger transplanted shrubs also face difficulty, because some of them will inevitably have been damaged when being dug up. They may need watering in dry periods until the roots can grow and penetrate out into the soil. Whatever the type of plant, the aim is to make the planting hole as welcoming as possible by introducing a mixture of soil and compost that small roots can easily work their way into, in order eventually to develop a network of strong roots.

IMPROVING THE SOIL

Most of us seek to improve our gardens by spending time and money on plants, but often gardeners are not aware of the need to nurture the soil, and how much the quality of the soil in our garden affects the growth of plants. Think of soil as the life blood of the garden, a living organism that sustains all living things and determines not only what grows but also how well it grows, and you will have some idea of its significance.

In nature there is great competition between plants for nutrients, space and light; stronger plants will survive over weaker, smaller ones, ensuring that they have enough resources to grow. There is an ebb and flow, with some plants fruiting and flowering at

Flowers grown for cutting.

certain times of the year, then dying back to a period of stillness. The soil is slowly replenished by falling leaves and organic debris that gradually decays and replenishes the soil.

The modern garden is a different story. We pack plants in closely together and expect all of them – including trees, shrubs, flowers, herbs, fruit, vegetables and hedges – to be both highly productive and ornamental. Unless simple measures to improve the fertility and structure of the soil are taken, such dense planting will rapidly deplete the soil of nutrients.

The levels of acidity or alkalinity (pH) in the soil may also determine what plants can be grown in your garden because it can affect how nutrients are taken up by the plant. Rhododendrons and Camellias thrive on acid soil, because the necessary nutrients are available to them, but when grown on an alkaline soil the nutrients remain locked up in the soil and unavailable. If you think that your soil is alkaline or acidic then it's worth testing it to establish the level and give you more information about what plants will thrive. This is easily done with a readily available soil testing kit (*see* Chapter 2).

Soil Structure

Soil structure describes the texture and consistency of soil, ideally for most plants, the soil will look dark brown, rich and crumbly. This formation allows the soil to hold onto water long enough for the plant to take up moisture and nutrients and then to gradually drain and not become waterlogged.

Of course, some plants don't suit these conditions, those of Mediterranean origin prefer light, well-drained soil that is relatively poor in nutrients and will fail if planted in rich soil. Conversely plants from boggy regions have adapted to those conditions and won't survive in light sandy soil. A knowledge of a plant's origin will indicate the most suitable conditions for a plant.

Soil Types

A basic understanding of the type of soil in your garden is necessary to know, not only what type of plants will be best suited to it, but also what steps can be taken to provide the best growing medium that has the appropriate level of nutrients in it.

Healthy soil produces healthy plants.

There are three main types of soil.

- *Clay* soil is heavy, easily water-logged in winter but slow to dry out in summer. It can be slow to warm up in spring because of the high water content, but this also results in it having a higher nutrient content than sandy or chalky soil.
- *Sandy* soil is light, well-drained and has a low nutrient content because they are leached from the soil as it drains. Its lightness makes it easier to work with and it warms up in the spring so seeds will germinate more quickly and plants root more quickly.
- *Chalky* soil is alkaline, light and well drained usually with just a thin layer of top soil so it lacks nutrients (*see* Chapter 6).

The good news is that there is a universal solution for improvement, whatever your type of soil. Add copious amounts of well-rotted manure or compost, annually as a mulch, preferably to a depth of 8–10cm. Use it also when planting by mixing it with garden soil when backfilling the planting hole. This improves the soil whatever its type, helping light soils to hang on to nutrients and moisture, and providing clay soils with a better structure so that they drain well and don't become waterlogged.

USING COMPOST

Compost is a confusing term that applies to many different planting mediums, including the bagged compost from garden centres used in hanging baskets and plant pots, often called multi-purpose compost. It also refers to John Innes potting composts that are slightly heavier, soil-based and used for potting-on plants into larger containers as they mature. These types of compost are specifically made for particular jobs and are not beneficial for improving soil in the garden.

Peat was commonly used in compost in the past, but we are discouraged from using it now as it is recognized that we are rapidly depleting this slowly produced resource, which also provides a valuable habitat in its local environment for specific wildlife. There are plenty of alternatives for gardeners to use, so check that any compost you buy does not contain peat.

If you buy compost look for those that are made from material rotted down over time from organic matter and referred to as 'organic compost' or 'soil improver'. But the best type of compost is made from material composted in your own garden – it's cheap, convenient, environmentally-friendly and you know exactly what's in it.

Making Your Own Compost

Try to avoid having bonfires in your garden; they release CO_2 into the atmosphere, and you miss the opportunity of converting a freely available by-product, such as leaves and selected garden waste, into a valuable resource for your garden.

Making compost is quite straightforward and easy to do, once a routine is established. The rewards will soon be apparent in your garden; it is hard to imagine how such benefits can result from a very straightforward process. Homemade compost is simply the best method of improving how your garden grows, and it's easy to see why compost is often referred to as black gold.

The process works on the simple principle that all living things decay and turn into humus (decomposed organic matter); bacteria feed on air that is incorporated into the compost (aerobic decomposition); and rich, crumbly nitrogen-rich compost is the result.

Do not use diseased or pest-affected plants, roots of perennial weeds such as dandelion or bindweed, or cooked food. If you have used any chemicals on your lawn, then wait two or three weeks before the clippings are included in the heap.

Leaf-Mould Compost

Fallen leaves are best treated separately from general garden compost, because they take longer to rot down into leaf-mould. This is a satisfying method of using up something commonly thought of as waste from your garden and turning it into a valuable commodity to improve the soil. All deciduous leaves rot down eventually, though some take longer than others; oak, alder and hornbeam are the quickest, whilst sycamore, beech, sweet-chestnut and horse-chestnut take the longest. Take care when collecting leaves in the autumn and winter from under hedges as hedgehogs and other creatures may be hibernating there.

If there are only a small number of fallen leaves in your garden each autumn, simply gather them up and store them in a plastic bin-bag; punch a few holes

Leaf-mould containers.

Garden Compost	
What You Can Compost	
Kitchen Waste	*Garden Waste*
Tea bags	Grass clippings
Coffee grounds	Pruning from soft plant matter (i.e. non woody)
Vegetable peelings	Spent vegetable plants
Egg boxes	Cut flowers
Cardboard tubes from kitchen paper	Small twigs
Banana skins and apple cores	Annual weeds
What You Cannot Compost	
From the Kitchen/House	*From the Garden*
Cooked food	Diseased plants
Meat	Pet litter
Fish	Branches
Coloured/coated paper	Plant material treated with chemicals
	Perennial weeds

in the sides with a garden fork, sprinkle the contents lightly with water, tie up the bag and store out of the way for a year or two. Check occasionally to stir up the contents and ensure that they haven't dried out, especially in the summer.

If your garden produces lots of leaves and you have space, then one or two custom-made compost bins will work well. Chicken-wire or some form of netting attached to four posts in the ground is all you need to make a container. Turn the contents very occasionally to mix the dryer sides into the centre to help the process along.

The resulting leaf-mould can be used either as a mulch or dug into the soil to improve its structure.

FERTILIZERS

The basic garden fertilizers are nitrogen, phosphorus and potassium, available in both organic and inorganic forms. Well-conditioned soils usually contain most of the nutrients that a plant needs to grow, but improving the level of nutrients may be necessary when growing hungry plants such as vegetables, perennials and annuals that make a lot of growth in one season.

Inorganic Fertilizer

The inorganic or chemical types are easily available from garden centres. Most have an information panel that gives the ratio of the content, expressed as N:P:K. (N is the chemical symbol for nitrogen, P for potassium and K for Phosphorus.)

A ratio of 7:7:7 is a balanced fertilizer with equal quantities of each, whereas 4:2:6 has a higher ratio of potassium and is used to encourage flowers and fruit. These inorganic fertilizers are produced in a form that is readily available to plants, and therefore they are quickly absorbed by the plant. But they also leech out quickly into the soil and are not of benefit for very long, so they have to be applied regularly and can be expensive.

Closely planted herbaceous plants perform well given liquid fertilizer.

Organic Fertilizer

Organic fertilizers originate from plant material such as seaweed and animal products, for example blood, fish and bone or pelleted chicken manure. Liquid fertilizers, such as comfrey or nettle tea, can be made from the bruised leaves of the plants that are then left to soak in a suitable lidded container. The resultant liquid is then diluted in water to produce a free, effective fertilizer. Organic fertilizers release their ingredients more slowly and usually need a period of time after application to break-down in the soil and become available to plants.

PREPARING THE SITE FOR PLANTING

Some weeks before you are ready to plant, maybe whilst you're choosing plants or waiting for the right time to plant, you can begin preparing the soil.

Dealing with Weeds

Determined, perennial weeds will need to be eradicated permanently or they will continue to reappear. They will be difficult to remove if they're growing through the new planting and will compete with the new plants for resources. Patience is needed if you garden organically because all the methods described take time to be effective.

Beware of trying to dig up intransigent weeds such as bindweed, because they can inadvertently be propagated when tiny pieces of root are left behind in the soil. The simplest method of eliminating weeds without using chemicals is to regularly cut them back; this weakens them, and eventually they just give up. An area of weeds can also be killed by covering with a strong material such as polythene, which blocks out light and rainfall and eventually kills them, although it has to be said that most materials do look unsightly.

If you are prepared to use chemicals then glyphosate is very effective, killing plants right back to their roots. Take care when applying it because it kills off any neighbouring plants that it also touches. It is only effective when used as the plant is growing, so shouldn't be used during the winter. Large plants can be cut back and reduced in size so that only a few leaves near the base have to be treated.

Whilst preparing the soil remember that although you can compost green waste, do not include the roots of weeds such as couch grass, bindweed, ground elder or other perennial weeds, or plants that have been treated with weed-killer.

Adding Fertilizer and Compost

Dig in some fertilizer, such as chicken manure pellets, a couple of weeks in advance of planting to give them time to break down into the soil. And if you don't have enough of your own compost, order plenty of soil-improving compost.

Moving Established Shrubs

It's unlikely that you're starting with a garden that is completely devoid of plants, so some of the preparation may include either moving some shrubs to a new place in your garden or giving them away.

There is no guarantee of survival when moving established plants, and some species such as roses and magnolias will object strongly, possibly by giving up completely. However, there are some measures that can be taken to reduce the risk, and choosing the right time to plant is one of them. The best time for moving deciduous plants is from late October to the middle of March. Evergreens are best moved during October when the soil still has some residual warmth, or late March when it is beginning to warm up again. When plants are dug up they will continue to lose moisture through their leaves but are unable to take up any through their roots, so avoid digging up plants on sunny and warm days in autumn.

Water the plant a few days before transplanting to let the roots take up water until they're settled in their new position; the moist soil will be better able to stick to the roots and protect them during the move.

Before digging up the plant prepare the new site by incorporating plenty of organic compost and forking through the soil in the base to help drainage. Make sure that the planting hole is wider and deeper than you estimate the size of the root-ball to be. Dig up the plant carefully, causing as little damage to the roots as possible and trying to keep some soil around the roots. Lift it onto some form of sheeting – damp sacking would be perfect – and cover the roots to prevent them drying out until the plant is happily planted in its new position.

If you can't replant it immediately – perhaps it's going to a new home elsewhere – either put it in a pot in the shade or dig a temporary hole or trench and gently heel it in so that the roots are covered until it can be moved to its permanent position. Many large tree nurseries have the specialist gear for moving mature trees and shrubs, and calling in a specialist could be the best choice if you have a mature tree that has to be moved.

PLANTING

As with most things in life, timing is important. In theory, planting all year round became possible with the advent of plastic pots, but in reality planting only at certain times of the year is sensible. Plants become stressed when planted during the summer or any time when it's warm and sunny; they struggle to take up enough water through an immature or damaged root system. A plant resorts to all sorts of measures to survive in a hostile environment; it may grow more slowly as fewer resources are available, or it can reduce its bulk by dropping some of its leaves so there's a smaller area of plant to look after. The result is a less attractive, smaller, weaker plant that has to be coaxed along and will be more susceptible to pests and diseases.

The ideal time for planting in the South of England is at the beginning of autumn, when the ground is still warm, but the weather is cooler and damper, putting less strain on newly planted plants. Failing this, anytime during the winter through to early spring is suitable, providing that the ground isn't water-logged or frozen. Light sandy soils offer more hospitable surroundings for planting in winter; heavy clay soil has a high water content that can be a cold, unfriendly place for new plants. Weather conditions won't be consistent at this time of year and there is a lot of variation in different parts of the country, so a certain amount of personal judgement will have to be used.

Having spent all that time and money getting this far, it makes sense to prepare well for planting so that your precious plants have the best possible chance to flourish. The soil will be ready, having been conditioned by the addition of copious amounts of well-rotted organic compost, and the weeds, especially the perennial type, will have been removed.

If plants have been delivered by a supplier unload them into a shady, sheltered spot and check their condition before you accept them and sign them off. They will probably need watering on arrival and checked again just before planting to ensure that the root-ball isn't dry. Immerse the whole plant pot in a bucket of water; air bubbles will rise to the surface; once this stops you know that any air pockets will have been replaced with water and that the root-ball is saturated.

If you're getting help with the planting, make sure that the gardeners know how to plant; this job is often seen as unskilled and may be delegated to someone who doesn't understand plants and how they grow. Correct planting techniques ensure that the plant grows well into a healthy specimen and is less susceptible to diseases and pests.

Shrubs

Potted Shrubs

Shrubs and trees may appear to be dormant during the winter, but their root systems continue to develop. If they are planted near springtime they will have had less time to extend their roots through the soil.

How to Plant a Shrub

Make sure the plant has been watered well in advance of planting.

Dig a hole large enough to accommodate the roots, using the pot as a guide and making the hole slightly deeper and wider than the root-ball. Leave enough room for the roots to spread out. Fork the sides and base of the planting hole.

Incorporate home-made or bought compost into the base of the planting hole and mix the remainder into the soil that came out of the planting-hole. Arrange the level of the soil so the plant can be planted at the same depth that it grew in the container – the mark can easily be seen on the stem.

Place the plant in the hole and begin to fill with soil around the roots, gently shaking the plant at first to ensure that the soil gets between the roots

Firm the soil gently with your heel to ensure that no large air pockets remain, but be careful not to compact the soil.

Water well on completion.

If they are planted during the summer, they struggle to survive and require regular watering to keep them alive. They will usually be weaker and more susceptible to pests and diseases. Mature plants are well adapted to the climate in this country, which can be very variable, and can survive through unexpected conditions. Given the right conditions, the roots' surface will develop beyond what is necessary for the plant's needs; this is a protective measure for adverse conditions, such as drought.

Bare-Root Shrubs

Bare-root plants are available in late autumn; they are sold without a pot or container, and root-balled plants are sold with a wire and hessian wrap around the roots. The biggest advantage is that they are less expensive than those in bought in plant pots, so they

Raspberry plants heeled in until they can be planted in their permanent position.

Bare-rooted fruit trees delivered by post.

are ideal if you need plants in large numbers for a new hedge. It is also a good way of buying fruit bushes and plants such as gooseberries and raspberries. These types of deciduous plants survive well in the autumn without being in a container and are ideal for sending by post. They should be unwrapped as soon as they arrive and heeled into a temporary place until they can be planted permanently. Order them at the end of the summer when there is plenty of choice of varieties.

When establishing bare-root plants microrhyzal funghi are a useful boost and are particularly reassuring to use when planting expensive specimens. To be completely effective the fungi must be sprinkled in contact with the roots at planting time. They form a large network of benign underground fungi that are naturally present in some soils and have a symbiotic relationship with the plant, absorbing carbohydrates from the roots and in turn increasing the roots' capacity for absorption of nutrients and moisture.

Interesting shapes of trees can be revealed in winter.

Trees

If the tree is to be planted in a lawn, remove all grass to a diameter of about 50cm; this prevents grass and weeds around the base of the tree competing for water and nutrients.

Make the planting hole about 10–15cm wider than the root-ball. Fork over the base of the hole; this will help drainage and root establishment. Dig in some chunky organic matter mixed with some fertilizer. Mix some compost with the soil that came out of the hole ready to re-fill the hole around the tree.

Now is the time to put in the tree stake; fix it firmly in place leaving about 60cm above the ground. A short stake allows some movement of the tree, which encourages root growth for stability. Take care not to damage the roots with the tree stake; it may be easier to use two small stakes either side of the tree with a cross-piece attached to them. Position the tree in the hole close to the stake, spreading out the roots. Ensure that the tree is planted at the same level as it grew in the nursery; this is easily seen as a line around the base of the tree.

Back-fill the planting hole gradually, shaking the tree gently to encourage the soil to work its way between the roots. Firm the soil with your heel.

Fix the tree to the stake with a proper rubber tree tie that loops around the tree and the stake in a figure of eight, so that the tree doesn't chafe against the stake.

Flexible irrigation tubes are available from specialist tree nurseries; they curl around the edge of the planting hole with the end sticking up above the soil so that the tree can be easily watered until it becomes well established.

As the tree grows check the tie regularly and loosen it as the stem grows and expands. Tree stakes are only an aid to help the tree until it is established and should be removed after the third season, so that the tree moves a little in the wind, developing strong, stabilizing roots.

Apply a mulch around the base of the tree to a depth of about 5cm, taking care not to cover the stem of the tree; this helps to retain moisture in the soil and reduce weed growth.

Herbaceous Plants and Grasses

Herbaceous plants are best planted at the end of the winter or early spring, as they don't like to have their roots in cold soil during the winter. Look out for small signs of growth as spring approaches; generally newly emerging weeds are a good sign that the soil is warming up ready for planting.

TOOLS

As with all crafts, garden tools become very personal belongings and are usually bought or inherited with great enthusiasm and noble intentions. The rows of shiny new tools hanging up on hooks in the garden centre are very appealing, until you look at the price tag, but garden tools should be an investment. The quantity and range of tools required will vary depending on the size and type of the garden, your physical

Garden Tools and Equipment

It's worth having good quality tools. They will last longer and make the job easier.

Pruning (keep blades sharp and oiled)

- Best quality secateurs with cross-over action
- Long-handled pruners
- Pruning knife
- Pruning saw and spare blades

Planting

- Good quality spade – stainless steel is light and gives a nice clean cut
- Fork of the right size and weight – a ladies' fork is smaller and lighter, useful for working in small areas, whatever your gender
- Small trowel and hand fork

Lawn

- Lawn mower – size appropriate to scale of lawns (regularly serviced)
- Nylon-line strimmer
- Lawn rake
- Lawn edging shears – long handled or electric
- Half-moon edger

Vegetable garden

- Dutch hoe (has a flattish blade) – used in a pushing forward and back motion for lightly breaking up the soil surface and chopping down small weeds
- Rake

General

- Watering can with a range of different sized roses
- Shears (kept sharp and oiled)
- Hedge trimmer – appropriate to size of hedges
- Hose pipe and reel, with good hose attachment
- Wheel barrow – consider folding wheel barrow if storage is limited
- Plastic trugs – these have endless uses: mixing compost or filled with water to dunk plants before planting
- Carrying sheets and bags for moving bulky waste
- Plant supports – a few different types
- Plant ties – jute and rose/tree ties
- Hammer and galvanized nails
- Good gardening gloves
- Sun hat and wellies
- Gardening reference books

New tools look very tempting, but they are an investment, so choose wisely.

strength and your gardening ability. Don't buy a huge hedge trimmer if you'll then require the services of a chiropractor after just ten minutes' use; and can you really justify the sit-on mower?

There are many sheds and cupboards filled with beautifully crafted garden tools that never see the light of day, whilst the pair of secateurs that never get put away because they are used nearly every day stay on the shelf in the kitchen. If this is the case the secateurs should be the best quality money can buy; have them serviced once a year, and your grandchildren will inherit them.

As with cooking or DIY gadgets most gardeners do not need a huge range of garden tools. A few carefully chosen items of the best quality you can afford will serve you better than a shed full of cheap ones. There are many companies that hire out garden tools and equipment, and this can be more economical for annually used items. Also there are no storage or maintenance issues.

AFTERCARE

Mulch

Mulch is a term used to describe various substances that are applied over the surface of the soil when planting is complete, and again on an annual basis, to reduce moisture loss and slow down weed growth. The annual mulch is best applied in early spring as the soil warms up and before it dries out. When applied at a depth of 10cm mulches can be very effective in keeping moisture in the soil. As a weed inhibitor organic mulches only inhibit annual weeds; the perennial types of weeds are too persistent, but they can be smothered by inorganic mulches such as shingle or plastic sheets.

The organic types, such as composted bark, have the added advantage that as they slowly decompose into the soil they improve its structure.

Mulches

Organic Mulches (these eventually decompose)		*Inorganic Mulches (do not decompose)*	
Home-made compost	Releases nutrients, improves soil structure	Gravel	Good at suppressing weeds, long lasting
Composted bark	Low nutrient release as it decomposes, improves soil structure	Polythene sheet	As above, unsightly but cheap
Cocoa shells	As above, but higher cost	Semi-permeable landscape fabric	Used over soil and under a mulch such as bark or gravel, will gradually decompose after many years
Well-rotted farmyard manure	As above, relatively cheap		

Watering

Correct watering, particularly if it's dry in early spring as plants start growing, is one of the key aspects of good establishment. Irrigate plants in the cool of the day during summer, and water thoroughly rather than light amounts that just encourage surface rooting. Soil that's been prepared with well-rotted compost will help the plant to hang on to every last drop of moisture so that the roots have time to soak it up.

Newly planted trees and shrubs need to establish quickly; this means being able develop their root system and settle into their new position. They will be off to a good start if you have followed all the above information and advice about plant selection, soil and preparation.

Using mulch in spring provides perfect soil conditions for herbaceous plants.

CREATIVE MAINTENANCE

Providing nutrients; weeding; protection from pests, weather and drought; pruning and supporting plants; looking after containers

Spring bulbs at Great Dixter.

Creating a planting scheme with expertise and flair and putting the plants in the ground successfully isn't the end of the story. The plants may be the right choice and perfect for the conditions in the garden, but what happens next? *They grow*, or at least they will try their very best to. They will increase in size sending out new growth with leaves, flowers, seeds and even fruit. They will get eaten by creatures, attacked by disease and battered by the weather. Then newcomers will invade your garden with its freshly dug soil

and, uninvited, take up residence. We call these weeds which, left unchecked, will clamber all over the new plants competing with them and probably winning because they are the tough guys in the neighbourhood. Those carefully chosen climbing plants and wall shrubs will ignore the fence or wall that you want them to cover and will head in the opposite direction, crawling along the ground or climbing over neighbouring plants. They may even prefer the look of the garden next door and flower on their side of the fence.

So obviously the solution is good old-fashioned gardening. For a planting design to really work well it takes knowledge, time and dedication to get the

OPPOSITE PAGE: **A mixed border at RHS Garden Wisley.**

planting established so it can flourish and develop. This chapter looks at how the long-term vision and health of the garden can be aided by ongoing garden maintenance which can be a very creative process, ensuring the success of the original design. A garden is never finished; it's always a work in progress.

THE GARDENER'S CALENDAR

Only a dedicated gardener will be ready and willing to go outside to work in the cold and damp of winter, but unless the ground is under snow, frozen or water logged this can be the busiest time in the gardener's calendar. Closing the door in mid-autumn and only venturing out again in mid-spring will not do! Many jobs can be done while the garden is 'asleep', and by mid-spring, when everything has started to wake up, it can be too late. Cutting back last year's fern fronds before the new ones start growing requires

timing and observation. Leave it too late and you can damage the beautiful unfurling fronds that are such a delight in early spring; remove them too early and frond buds are vulnerable to frost.

Planting, moving and pruning can all be carried out through the autumn and winter. In the spring there is propagating, sowing seeds and re-potting containers to do. Leave all this until the end of spring, and the jobs are too numerous and it may be too late because everything has started growing again. There is however, a good argument for not clearing gardens before the end of winter, as dead foliage can provide shelter and seed for wildlife and can protect tender shoots and buds from cold and frost.

So timing is critical, and you need to keep a close eye on the weather and those first signs of growth in the garden; remember if weed seed is germinating it means the soil has warmed up. Invest in a basic weather station with a maximum/minimum thermometer and rain gauge to measure the changes in your garden, and use the weather services on the internet to get information in advance.

Newly emerged epimedium leaves in early spring.

JOBS	SEPT	OCT	NOV	DEC	JAN	FEB	MARCH	APRIL	MAY	JUNE	JULY	AUG
Shrubs	dead head roses prune summer flowering shrubs	dead head roses prune summer flowering shrubs	plant any new shrubs		prune roses	cut back old fern fronds prune	prune winter flowering shrubs winter flowering shrubs	plant any tender shrubs or herbs cut back sage		prune spring flowering shrubs	dead head roses prune early summer flowering shrubs	dead head roses
Trees					prune pear tree		cut back bay tree	trim olive tree				
Climbers	tie in new growth				prune & train climbing roses check wires on fences	cut back summer clematis check for snail damage	cut back winter flowering climbers	tie in new growth	tie in new growth	dead head roses tie in new growth	dead head roses tie in new growth	dead head roses tie in new growth
Perennials						remove dead stems & tidy	install supports lift and split perennials	plant new perennials	dead head	dead head	dead head check stakes	dead head cut back early plants
Bulbs		plant spring bulbs tidy bulbs in pots	order summer bulbs		look out for Snowdrops emerging	watch out for snail damage on bulb leaves		plant summer bulbs check bulbs in pots			order spring bulbs for autumn deliver	
Lawn		feed lawn	take mower to be serviced	clear dead leaves off lawn			begin mowing weekly if grass is growing	sow grass seed on bare patches	feed lawn	mow weekly	mow weekly	mow weekly
Pond		remove dead leaves	clean out pump			look out for frog spawn	tidy plants and clear debris	buy new pond plants			check water levels & remove pond weed	check water levels & remove pond weed
Compost bin		empty liquid from wormery base	wrap up wormery			unwrap wormery	empty wormery				empty liquid from wormery base	
Containers	plant up for winter	remove saucers	protect with bubble wrap			decide on summer bedding & order	remove bubble wrap. Top up old containers with new compost, replant pots	plant up for summer replace saucers & rearrange	feed roses & shrubs		feed roses & shrubs	
Irrigation	disconnect irrigation system & remove automatic timers		wrap up outside tap & pipes before frost			check irrigation system	clean out water butts	reconnect irrigation for pots		reconnect irrigation for borders		
Pests	snail hunt	snail hunt	snail hunt					snail hunt look out for greenfly	snail hunt	snail hunt look out for greenfly		
Design	take photos for future reference				plan changes to planting for this year			take photos for future reference	take photos for future reference	take photos for future reference	take photos for future reference	take photos for future reference
Wildlife	bird feeders clean out nest boxes	bird feeders & insect boxes	bird feeders	bird feeders	bird feeders	bird feeders	bird feeders & check fox deterrent	bird feeders	bird feeders	bird feeders	bird feeders	bird feeders
Tools			take secateurs and loppers to be sharpened	tidy shed & add tools to Xmas list	get mower serviced							

Make a personalized gardening calendar to help organise jobs through the year.

PROVIDING NUTRIENTS

We have talked about the importance of understanding the geology of your soil in other chapters but here we will look at how to maintain the health of your soil. Nearly all garden soil can be improved but how much improvement is needed will depend largely on what is to be grown.

A low-maintenance scheme of trees and shrubs will want some help to get started, provided they are right for the conditions. Once they are established they should manage quite happily with the occasional mulch of good compost around their roots.

If the scheme is made up of mixed shrubs, herbaceous perennials and an assortment of different grasses and bulbs, the soil is being asked to do a lot of work looking after all those different needs. Some plants will want more food and moisture than their neighbours; some will want less. The aim is to regularly put back nutrients which the plants have used and the rain has leached out, but also to maintain good soil structure. The best way to do this is to use a mulch of good garden compost and, if necessary, plant fertilizers (*see* Chapter 8).

The result of improving the soil means plants can access the nutrients easier. But how much food do established plants need? It is possible to over-feed established plants; this can result in weak leggy growth, making them prone to disease and poor flowering, or it may just encourage them to grow too big. Some plants thrive on poor soil and need to be starved in order to flower well, such as nasturtiums and many rock plants. The type of soil makes a big difference; for example sandy, well-draining soil needs more maintenance than nutrient-rich clay. If you have chosen plants that are not really suitable for the conditions in your garden, they will require more long-term maintenance in order to help them thrive.

PROTECTION

Gardening is about tending and nurturing, but it's also about protecting the plants from competition from weeds and attack from pests and disease as well as extremes of weather. Establishing a balance will allow nature to do much of this for you, but a garden will never be a totally natural environment, so for the best results plan to work with nature rather against it.

Weeds

Weeds are only plants growing in the wrong place. They tend to be very adaptable, strong growing and successful at spreading themselves around, but then so do a lot of cultivated plants. Valuable garden plants such as alstromaria or crocosmia can be too invasive for small gardens, and may be classed as a weed.

How then do you tell which is a weed and which is a garden plant? The type of weeds commonly found in your garden will depend on where you live and the growing conditions; if the weeds are growing well, then so should the other plants in your garden. Plant societies and local gardening groups are very useful

Lysimachia clethroides is a beautiful herbaceous perennial but can be too vigorous for some gardens.

for sharing information specific to your area, and the RHS has an excellent advice service. The internet can also be used to help identify unknown plants. A flora such as *The Concise British Flora in Colour* by W. Keble Martin is an essential book for any new gardener.

Weeds can be introduced into the garden in many different ways, the most obvious being seeds blown by the wind or carried by birds, but many weeds also come from the soil of newly introduced plants. Weeds that are allowed to flower and set seed will spread, so don't let them. If you don't have time to pull up the dandelions, at least remove their flowers to stop them seeding everywhere.

Deter weed seed from germinating on bare soil and newly planted areas by applying a mulch of bark or compost. Remember – bare soil will always need weeding, so cover it up with either plants or a mulch of bark chips or compost.

There is, however, a drawback to having a weed-free garden: you don't get any self-seeded treasures or plants for free. New seedlings may be weeds or they may be useful plants, and knowing which is which requires experience. If you are not sure, try letting a seedling get to a size where you can identify it, then if it's a weed pull it up. If it turns out to be a useful plant, then leave it alone, move it or pot it up and grow it on.

Pests and Diseases

A healthy garden will have a good bio-diversity with a range of plants which attract and support animals and insects, creating a natural balance. Using chemicals will upset this balance and could simply lead to another problem. Most pests are food for many birds, frogs and beneficial insects, and a good gardener is patiently willing to accept that the wildlife may sometimes eat the garden. Healthy, strong growing plants can withstand an attack from pests and diseases much better than those that are damaged or weak due poor growing conditions or old age, and this should be addressed first. Observing and monitoring your garden on a regular basis will help you decide whether to take action to help a plant under attack or leave nature to get on with it.

Extreme Weather

Cold and Heat

How much protection your garden needs from extreme weather will depend on your location; a sheltered city garden will have very different needs to an exposed site on the east coast of Britain. As mentioned all through this book if the planting is suitable for the normal conditions in your garden you shouldn't have too much trouble, but extremes can happen.

In the case of a hard frost, horticultural fleece can be used in an emergency to protect vulnerable plants or tender flower buds, and a deep mulch of bark chips or straw will help prevent roots being frozen in the ground. Deep snow is very heavy and can easily break branches, so try to remove it from small trees and shrubs if possible. Smaller plants will be protected under an insulating layer of snow, so leave them covered. Don't walk on lawns when the ground is frozen or waterlogged as you will damage them.

Heat can also be a problem, but will only really affect those plants which prefer cool damp conditions such as rhododendrons and camellias. Most plants will recover even if they look very unhappy, and again mulching the ground will help to keep the soil moist.

Strong winds and gales can do a great deal of damage to any garden, and if your area is susceptible make sure you keep up to date with the maintenance of tree stakes and plant supports. Be vigilant about looking at the weather reports and try to be as prepared as possible for any extreme weather conditions.

Drought

Drooping leaves are the first sign of a plant that is suffering from lack of water; they may then become brown around the edges or fall off. The plant's best defence against serious drought is to drop all its leaves, but healthy, well-established plants should recover.

If you have stored rain water use a very slow trickling hose pipe at the base of the plant, rather than a quick splash to get the water deep down into the roots. For plants in small containers soak pots in a bucket of water until they become heavy, and use saucers under larger pots which will act as a reservoir.

A well-established garden should need little watering, and lawns recover easily from drought.

Mulching will prevent water loss so use bark, compost or gravel on top of the soil in the garden and in containers. Plants that have been in a container for a few years may have become root bound, which means there is little soil left, only roots. The plant will begin to struggle, so either put it in the ground or into a larger container with new compost.

Only newly planted ground needs irrigating, and established plants should manage without any watering even in dry weather providing they are the right plants for the conditions (*see* Chapter 8 for information on caring for newly planted gardens.) Over-watering little and often will stop plants from establishing a deep root system, making them less able to withstand drought. An established mixed border may have new planting each year as perennials are lifted, divided and replanted, but if this is done in the spring or autumn rather than the summer, watering can be kept to a minimum. Only water after the sun has gone down in the evening to allow the soil to soak up the moisture and prevent evaporation. Sometimes if a plant is stressed due to disease or damage it may require extra water to help it back to full health.

Tap water is expensive and requires a great deal of energy to produce so using it to water a garden is a luxury which is now becoming less acceptable. The alternative is storing rain water and there are now a great many ways to do this whatever the size of your garden. It is also possible to use grey water from washing machines and baths but this must to be done correctly to prevent contaminating your garden.

Watering established lawns is also unnecessary in the UK. If there is a drought they will require unrealistic amounts of water to keep them green which is neither economic nor environmentally sound. Lawns may look dead and brown in a hot summer, but so will everyone else's and they will recover after the first good shower of rain. As with all the other planting in the garden, good lawn maintenance will help it survive a drought.

DIVIDING PERENNIALS

Most perennial plants will need to be lifted, divided and replanted after three or four years depending on the rate of growth, and this encourages the plant to make new, healthy stems which will produce more flowers. This usually results in having more of the plant than you need to refill the space they came out of, and the surplus can be used elsewhere in the garden or given away.

The techniques for lifting and dividing vary depending on the type of plant, and a good reference book will give you this information. The ideal time for lifting and dividing is in spring or autumn depending on how hardy the plant is. Tender or drought-tolerant plants such as iris are best divided in the spring, as they have the summer to get established again before the cold of winter.

PRUNING

Good pruning techniques are integral to successful, long-term planting design and essential for retaining the shapes (discussed in Chapter 6). Poor pruning can result in all the shrubs becoming the same generic blob or bun shape, with no character or grace and

Repeat flowering roses like this 'Elizabeth of Glamis' will continue to bloom for many months if regularly dead-headed.

often no flowers. All pruning should aim to retain or enhance the natural shape of the shrub.

The main reason for pruning is to remove any dead, diseased or damaged branches or stems, and this is all most trees and shrubs will need, given ample space to grow. If pruning is required it's important to think about how your actions will affect the growth of the plant and what it is you are trying to achieve. In the wild all plants experience damage at some time, whether it's from animals, wind or falling rocks, and nature has adapted to cope with this so the plant can survive and continue to grow. By cutting a stem or branch you will set off a chemical reaction which starts the process of healing, and how the plant reacts depends on where the cut is made.

Dead-heading

Dead-heading or removing faded flowers is also a form of pruning. There are three reasons for removing faded flowers: (1) to encourage the plant to produce new flowers, (2) to prevent the plant from putting its energy into making unwanted fruit and seeds, and (3) to keep the appearance of the plant tidy. At the end of the day it is still pruning.

Reshaping

All plants will naturally grow towards the light but essentially their tendency is to grow symmetrically, and this is what we are trying to achieve when pruning (unless training climbers or wall shrubs). If a plant has grown into an awkward shape, before pruning ask the question why? Is it because of lack of space, lack of light or has it been damaged by weather or animals? Pruning in these cases may only be a short-term solution. If the problem is lack of light or space the plant may need to be moved or replaced. If it has been damaged by weather or animals the problem may reoccur so look to prevention. When reshaping a plant, you are usually trying to achieve an open, symmetrical structure with no crossing or awkward-looking stems or branches.

Try to achieve an open symmetrical structure.

Established hedges and topiary need regular trimming to keep them in shape – how often will depend on the growing conditions and the type of plant, but also how tidy you want the plant to look. Box and yew may be trimmed lightly twice a year, once in the spring and again in mid summer. Do not leave cutting evergreen hedges or topiary too late in the autumn as pruning then will encourage new growth that may be damaged by the cold in winter. The best time to reshape hedges is at the end of winter or beginning of spring when the new growth will help to disguise the resulting bare stems. Large hedges can be a big maintenance job, and expensive if professional help is required, so this needs to be considered carefully at the planning stage.

pruned hard every few months in order to keep it in bounds then you must ask yourself whether it's the right plant in the right place? The plant will sooner or later become weak and will certainly fail to flower. Most healthy shrubs can tolerate light pruning once or twice a year.

Timing

When to prune is often the most common question, and the answer will depend on the type of plant and what you are trying to achieve. Are you trying to improve flowering and fruiting, or increase stem and leaf growth or both?

Rejuvenating

Most gardens will have some existing shrubs which will be incorporated into the new scheme, but these may be old and in need of rejuvenating. Many established shrubs can benefit from being pruned hard, encouraging old stems to be replaced with new, stronger growth. When you cut into a branch or stem, you will cause the plant to react, and hard pruning can cause the plant to grow back more vigorously, so decide if this is what you want to happen. Sometimes only removing one third of the old growth will give tired old shrubs a new lease of life while keeping some control of the size.

Reducing

Often we prune plants because they have grown beyond their allotted space. If a plant has to be

---

When to Prune?

- **Spring flowering plants:** Prune immediately after flowering in the *spring*, as these produce flower buds on stems made the previous summer.
- **Summer flowering:** Prune immediately after flowering in the *summer*, as these produce flower buds on stems made earlier in the spring.
- **Autumn flowering:** Prune the *following spring* as soon as the danger of frost is past, as these produce flower buds on stems made in early summer.
- **Winter flowering:** Prune the *following spring* as soon as the danger of frost is past, as these produce flower buds on stems grown during the previous summer and autumn.

following spring when the worst of the cold weather is over.

You can prune some hardy shrubs such as roses in the middle of winter when they are dormant and therefore unlikely to produce new growth, but if you are not sure then leave them until the spring. Some plants grown for their attractive winter stems such as cornus (dogwood) tend to have the best colour on new wood, so encourage these by removing all the old wood in spring just as the new stems start to grow.

Some plants in warm sheltered positions never stop flowering, and you have to judge the best time to prune if it has outgrown its space. Vigorous climbers such as the passion flower *Passiflora caerulea* and *Solanum jasminoides* are good examples of this, and at some point you just have to be brutal and remove growth with flowers and buds in spring or early summer.

How to Prune

Always use the correct tools. Use sharp, good quality secateurs, preferably with by-pass (scissor-like) action for thin stems, and loppers or long-handled pruners for thicker stems. Use a curved pruning saw for very

Red cornus stems in winter.

Flowering plants seem to be the most confusing. One simple rule to follow is to only prune after the plant has finished flowering. If you prune a plant just before it starts flowering, you may cut off the stems carrying the flower buds. If you are not sure when the flowering season is, either wait to see what happens and make a note, or if you know the name of the plant look in a reference book or on the plant label.

Pruning too late in the autumn will encourage tender new growth which will then be vulnerable to cold and frost, so leave late-autumn flowering plants such as fuchsias and hydrangeas until early the

Always cut just above a new outward-facing bud.

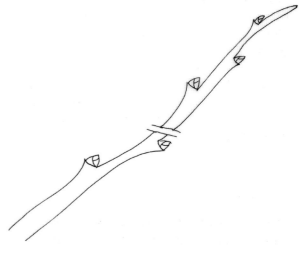

Some large shrubs like abelia can be reduced and rejuvenated in stages.

thick or tough branches, and shears for hedges. Trying to prune stems which are too thick will shorten the life of the tools and result in an untidy cut which can cause die-back or encourage disease.

Some plants can be cut down to the ground and will happily grow back, but some can die or become weak if cut back too hard. If you are not sure how hard to prune then follow this simple rule. Do not cut further down than where you see new growth forming. Lavender and most hardy herbs, for example, may not produce new growth from old wood (that which is more than two years old) so should only be lightly trimmed.

Many shrubs will flower best on new stems that are only one or two years old, and these can have a pruning regime. Each year remove the older stems from low down the plant, and new stems will grow to replace them. Some old or neglected shrubs can be given a new lease of life in stages by removing one third of the old growth in the first year, another third in the second year and the remaining third in the final year. This way you can still enjoy some flowers without having to wait for the whole plant to grow back if you cut all the stems down to the ground in one go.

CLIMBING PLANTS AND WALL SHRUBS

Climbing plants and wall shrubs probably need the most regular attention in a garden, even if they are

A rose trained up a post.

self clinging such as ivy and climbing hydrangea. Left alone they will send out stems all over the place or try to make a large unruly bush. With time and knowledge a well-trained climber should be an asset to a garden rather than a badly behaved thug. Established climbers such as wisteria or jasmine can grow at a terrific rate and if left unchecked can cause significant damage to a property, pulling down drain pipes and gutters or getting under roof tiles. Rambling roses can turn a pergola into a hazard if thorny stems are allowed a free rein. A well-trained climber will flower more profusely with a better display; for example wisteria flowers should dangle elegantly from horizontal branches rather than getting lost in a tangle of stems and leaves.

True Climbers

True climbing plants have specially adapted stems which allow them to climb. In the wild their stems would scramble up a tree or over a large shrub to reach the light, where they would produce flowers and leaves. The lower stems would become bare, because their role is to support the top growth. When a true climber is grown against a fence or wall, it will treat this support as if it were a tree and scramble to the top where it will produce flowers. The lower stems will become unsightly bare 'legs', and space is needed to grow another plant in front to disguise them, so designing the planting spaces large enough is essential.

There are various methods climbers adopt to enable them to climb. Honeysuckle and clematis have twining stems and leaf stalks, hydrangea and ivy are self-clinging by means of sucker-like growths or aerial roots along the stems, and roses use their thorns as hooks to grab onto a support. Many will rely on the wind to send their stems over a support in a totally random fashion, but their main aim is to grow towards the light.

Wall Shrubs

Wall shrubs such as pyracantha and ceanothus are often confused with true climbers, but if these shrubs are planted in the ground and left untrained they will make a large shrub or small tree, whereas if they are planted next to a support and trained against it they become a wall shrub. A great many shrubs can be trained in this way, but they require regular work to make this happen; some can be bought ready trained against a framework, which makes the job much easier.

A wall shrub is less likely to have 'bare legs' as it will still produce leaves and flowers on lower stems, depending on the variety, but only if it has been trained from a young plant; a shrub with a conventionally established framework may be difficult to retrain. The plants which are easiest to train against a support are those with long stems which are soft

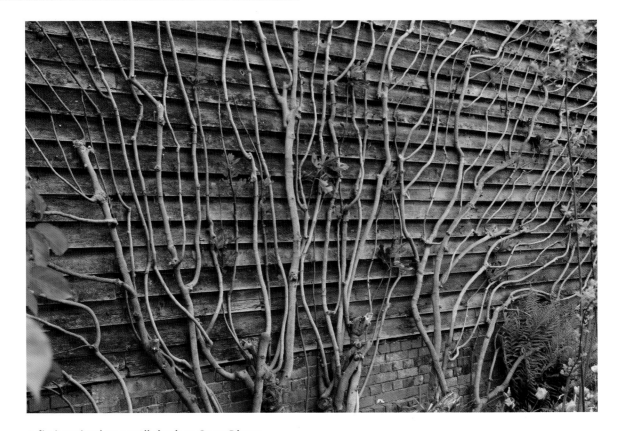

A fig is trained as a wall shrub at Great Dixter.

and pliable when young and respond well to being pruned, freely sending out new stems from the base of the plant.

Training Climbers and Wall Shrubs

When a climber or wall shrub is first planted it will take about three to five years to establish its permanent framework, and during this time will need regularly tying in rather than pruning. Once a good framework is in place, new flowering stems are then pruned back to this each year. The size you allow the framework to reach is dependant on the space it is occupying. If the space is limited then you restrict the size of the framework. A good example of this can be seen in vineyards where the vines are reduced back to just one or two main stems each year, yet they still produce lots of grapes. It is also a good idea to limit

the height of the framework to where you can easily reach without having to install scaffolding each year to prune it. Neglecting to limit its size will result in damaged drainpipes and gutters.

The shape of the framework depends on the type of plant being trained, but it can make a big difference to the number of flowers produced. With roses for example, if a stem is allowed to grow vertically it will only flower at the top; if it is trained horizontally it will send out flowering stems all along its length and each year those flowered stems are cut back to the horizontal framework. Once a framework is established the plant can be kept rejuvenated by allowing two or three new stems to replace the old ones every couple of years.

Knowing how much pruning each type of plant requires can be confusing, but a good reference book or specialist publication should help you acquire the necessary knowledge for all the different plants in your garden. Once you understand how a plant grows, you will find pruning and training is no more than logical common sense and just like solving a puzzle; it's easy when you know how.

STAKING AND SUPPORTING

In the wild plants will only grow where the conditions are right for them and where there is enough space. In a garden we bring plants together from many different environments and expect them to grow cheek by jowl with often less than perfect conditions. On top of that we then want them to look perfect and perform better than what they might achieve in the wild, so small wonder that staking and supporting is

---

Some Suggested Plant Supports

Bamboo canes cheap, useful for tall single stems such as hollyhocks or delphiniums, but unsightly

Metal poles strong and durable, useful for emergencies

Preformed plastic or metal supports many to choose from, metal lasts longer than plastic, a selection of different types is useful, good quality metal supports can be a good investment

Pea sticks free or very cheap, effective and discreet, they only last one or two seasons so find good, regular supply

Shrub prunings free, very effective if available in large enough pieces and quantities

Withies willow or hazel whips can be woven and tied together to create a range of useful supports, particularly for plants which overhang lawn edges

Metal wire should only be used for support wires on fences or walls, never as plant ties as they cut into the stem

Natural jute best material for tying plant stems

---

sometimes needed. This is particularly true in small gardens where plants will often produce longer, softer stems in their need to compete for light. The advantage of a well-planned mixed border is that sturdy shrubs can give support to soft-stemmed perennials and other plants, reducing the need to use stakes. But the timely use of plant supports can make a huge difference, allowing you to enjoy a plant at the peak of perfection rather than lamenting over broken stems and drooping flowers.

There are many different types of plant supports; some are expensive and some are free. What you use will depend on personal preference and budget. Whichever types you use, the critical aspect is timing; once a plant has blown over or been battered by the wind it is probably too late to be rescued. Install plant supports before they are needed and they will disappear, hidden by the foliage as the plants grow up through them. Visiting National Trust and RHS gardens where this kind of maintenance is carried out to perfection is an excellent way of learning how to stake plants properly. In early spring when the herbaceous perennials are just starting to show you will see a variety of different methods being used way ahead of their being needed by the plants.

CONTAINERS

Growing plants in containers requires all the same theories as growing plants in the ground in terms of design and choosing the right plants for the conditions. However keeping a plant healthy long term requires a little extra work. They will have a smaller root run and less soil so are totally reliant on what's in the pot to sustain them.

Never use soil straight from the garden in a container. For one reason the balance of micro organisms will be disturbed, and pests and disease in the soil may affect the health of the plant. If possible use fresh potting compost, which should be sterile (heat treated) and free from any contamination. There is a range of different types depending on what you are growing, whether it's germinating seeds or rooting

Lilies can be grown in unobtrusive black plastic pots and positioned in the border when they are flowering, to add extra colour and scent.

Supports for herbaceous perennials have been made using fresh pea sticks, which have been pushed into the ground and woven around the plants.

cuttings, but for permanent planting in containers a loam-based John Innes formula compost is recommended.

If you want a plant to thrive in a container for more than a couple of seasons you need to replenish the compost each year. You can do this by scraping off the top 5–10cm of soil and replacing it with good fresh potting compost along with a slow-release fertilizer. The best time to do this is in the spring when the plant is bursting back to life after the winter. Covering the compost with a mulch of gravel or bark chips will prevent weed seed germinating and reduce the risk of the container drying out.

It is much easier to control the drainage in a container than in the ground. If you are growing a plant which needs the compost to be damp, place a saucer under it to act as a reservoir. If the plant likes it dry, raise the container up onto feet. Either way the water must always be able to drain through or it will become stagnant and the plant will die.

Well thought out and maintained containers can be a huge asset to any planting design, whether they are seasonal or long term. If the container itself is very ornamental, try to keep the planting simple or the effect can be overwhelming. Alternatively, if the container is very plain, the planting can be as exuberant and elaborate as you like and the pot will simply disappear. Containers can be experimental without affecting the long term plan, or used to extend the range of growing conditions in a garden. They can offer growing spaces where there were none or add a welcome burst of seasonal colour and texture to any planting scheme.

OPPOSITE PAGE: When a passion for growing plants is combined with a love of gardening a beautiful garden can be the result... and when a passion for design is combined with a love of plants and gardening the results can be breathtaking.

PLANT CATEGORIES AND DEFINITIONS

CATEGORIES OF STRUCTURAL PLANTS

Architectural leaved plants are plants with no defined overall shape but distinctive and even dramatic shaped leaves.

Evergreen ferns are neither shrubs nor perennials, but an ancient group of plants going back to prehistoric times. They have fronds that look like leaves and no flowers.

Evergreen grasses, rushes, sedges and bamboo all belong to a huge family of diverse plants that are often confused with each other. They can range from just a few inches to over twelve feet in height.

Evergreen ground cover plants are used to cover the ground and form a dense carpet.

Evergreen perennials are plants that do not produce woody stems. They live for more than two years and produce flowers annually. Evergreen perennials keep their leaves and non-woody stems through the winter but they will normally be replaced with new growth in the spring.

Hedges are shrubs that respond well to being trimmed and are planted close together usually in rows. Hedges play an important role as the green walls of a garden.

Key plants have a permanent, distinctive shape and are usually evergreen. They can be shrubs, perennials, ferns or grasses.

Semi-evergreen shrubs may lose a proportion of their leaves in winter, depending on how extreme the climate.

Trees whether deciduous or evergreen bring a strong vertical element to a garden and are always structural.

CATEGORIES OF ORNAMENTAL PLANTS

Aquatics and marginal plants – aquatics are plants that have adapted to living with their roots and stems permanently in water and cannot survive long on dry land. Marginal plants like to have only their roots in wet mud and grow in the edges of ponds. They can be any type of plants, such as perennials, shrubs, grasses or ferns and even trees.

Climbing plants and wall shrubs – climbing plants require something to grow over and are called true climbers, whereas wall shrubs are plants that do not need support unless they are trained against a wall or fence.

Culinary plants include fruit, vegetables and herbs.

Deciduous ferns, grasses, rushes and sedges have stems, fronds (in the case of ferns) and leaves, all of which die back completely in the winter, producing new growth in the spring.

Deciduous shrubs will lose all their leaves in winter and will be left with bare branches that may be ornamental.

Fillers are plants used to fill the gaps between permanent planting as it matures. The following groups of plants can all be used as fillers.

- **bulbs, corms, tubers and rhizomes** are also used as herbaceous perennials.
- **annuals** are plants that germinate in the spring, produce flowers in the summer, set seed and die before the winter. Short-lived perennials are also sometimes classed as annuals because they live less than two or three years.
- **Biennials** are plants that germinate and produce a plant in the first year, then flower, set seed and die in the second year.
- **Tender perennials** originate from warm climates such as South Africa, South America and the Mediterranean. They are often classed as annuals when grown in countries with cold winters because they are too tender to survive through to the following year unless protected from the cold.

Herbaceous perennials have stems and leaves that all die back completely in the winter, producing new growth in the spring.

Rock plants and alpines are small plants that have adapted to growing amongst rocks and dry stony soil, or ground cover plants that can tolerate a wide range of conditions.

LIST OF PLANTS

The following is an at-a-glance guide to the various conditions in which particular plants will thrive, together with a note of the shape of the plant to help you in planning your garden. We have used italic text here to denote an acid-loving plant.

DRY SHADE ....**SHAPE**

Shrubs

Buddleja .... arching
Choisya .... dome
Corylus (Hazel) .... arching
Cotoneaster................................... arching
Elaeagnus ebbingii........................... dome
Euonymus .... dome
Ilex (Holly)....................................... dome
Lonicera (Honeysuckle)................. arching
Mahonia .... column
Nandina domestica .... column
Philadelphus.................................. arching
Potentilla .... dome
Prunus .... dome
Rubus (Ornamental Bramble) .... arching
Sambucus (Elder)........................... arching
Sarcoccoca .... dome
Skimmia.. dome
Viburnum .... various

Conifers

Juniper .... column
Yew.. column

Perennials

Alchemilla mollis.............................. dome
Anemone japonica.......................... column
Aquilegia alpina............................. column
Astelia chathamica............................ dome

Bergenia cordifolia............................. dome
Euphorbia robbiae .... column
Geranium .... dome
Helleborus .... dome
Heuchera.. dome
Lamium maculatum .... spreading
Phormium .... arching
Pulmonaria .... spiky dome
Tiarella cordifolia .... dome

Ferns & grasses

Asplenium scolopendrium .... arching
Dryopteris affinis........................... arching
Luzula.................................... spiky dome
Ophiopogon planiscarpus.....................spreading

Climbers

Garrya elliptica
Hedera (Ivy)
Hydrangea petiolaris
Lonicera
Pileostegia
Rubus
Chaenomeles speciosa

DRY SUN....................................**SHAPE**

Shrubs

Abutilon vitifolium var. album .... arching
Buddleja.. arching
Caryopteris x clandonensis .... column
Ceanothus...................................... dome
Ceratostigma.................................... dome
Cistus .... dome
Convolvulus cneorum........................ dome
Cytisus.. arching
Deutzia... arching

Hebe	dome
Hibiscus	column
Lavandula	dome
Leptospermum	column
Perovskia	arching
Philadelphus	arching
Physocarpus	arching
Rosa rugosa	arching
Rosemary	column
Salvia (Sage)	dome
Syringa vulgaris	arching

Perennials

Achillea	dome
Artemisia	various
Dianthus	dome
Diascia	spreading
Echinops	column
Eryngium alpinum	column
Foeniculum (Fennel)	arching
Iris	arching
Lychnis	arching
Sedum	various
Stachys	spreading
Verbena	column

Grasses

Cortaderia selloana	arching
Festuca glauca	spiky dome
Helictotrichon sempervirens	arching
Miscanthus	arching

Climbers & wall shrubs

Abutilon
Actinidia kolomikta
Hedera/Ivy
Jasminum officinale
Passiflora caerulea
Parthenocissus
Pyracantha
Solanum
Climbing Roses
Myrtus communis

MOIST SHADE ....SHAPE
Shrubs

Acer	arching
Camellia	column
Cornus	dome
Corylus (Hazel)	arching
Cotoneaster	arching
Crinodendron hookerianum	arching
Elaeagnus ebbingii	column
Fatsia japonica	arching
Fuchsia	arching
Hydrangea	dome
Lonicera	various
Mahonia	column
Phyllostachys (Bamboo)	column
Pieris 'Forest Flame'	dome
Rhododendron/Azalea	dome
Sambucus	arching

Perennials

Ajuga	spreading
Dicentra	arching
Digitalis – biennial	column
Epimedium	spreading
Hemerocallis – semi shade	arching
Heuchera	dome
Zantedeschia	arching

Ferns & Grasses

Asplenium scolopendrium	arching
Carex	spiky dome
Dryopteris affinis	arching
Matteuccia struthiopteris	arching
Pennisetum orientale	dome
Polystichum setiferum	arching

Climbers & wall shrubs

Chaenomeles speciosa
Climbing Roses
Crinodendron hookerianum
Garrya elliptica
Hedera/Ivy
Hydrangea petiolaris
Lapageria rosea

Lonicera henryi
Lonicera x americana
Parthenocissus
Pyracantha

MOIST SUN ....SHAPE
Shrubs
Camellia ....column
Hydrangea.................................... dome
Magnolia ....arching
Roses .... arching
Euphorbia...................................... column
Potentilla .... dome
Corylus (Hazel) .... arching
Salix (Willow) .... arching
Osmanthus.................................... dome
Ilex .... dome
Fuchsia .... arching

Perennials
Ligularia .... arching
Filipendula.................................... arching
Iris sibirica .... column
Lysimachia.................................... column
Lythrum salicaria .... arching
Penstemon .... various
Rodgersia .... arching
Thalictrum..................................... column
Gunnera manicata......................... dome

Ferns & Grasses
Carex .... spiky dome
Cortaderia selloana....................... arching
Miscanthus.................................... arching
Uncinia.. arching

Climbers & wall shrubs
Chaenomeles speciosa
Clematis montana
Climbing Roses
Crinodendron hookerianum
Garrya elliptica
Hedera/Ivy
Hydrangea petiolaris
Jasminum officinale

Lonicera henryi
Lonicera periclymenum
Lonicera x tellmanniana
Magnolia grandiflora
Parthenocissus henryana
Pyracantha 'Mohave'
Solanumn crispum 'Glasnevin'
Solanum jasminoides 'Album'

COASTAL ....SHAPE
Trees
Acer... arching
Arbutus .... arching
Crataegus (Hawthorn) .... dome
Ilex .... dome
Juniper .... column
Oak .... dome
Pine... column
Poplar.. column
Salix .... arching
Sorbus... dome

Shrubs
Arundinaria.................................... column
Callistemon .... dome
Calluna .... dome
Ceanothus .... dome
Choisya .... dome
Cistus .... dome
Cotoneaster.................................. arching
Cytisus.. arching
Elaeagnus .... column
Erica ....spreading
Fuchsia .... arching
Griselinia .... column
Hippophae (Sea Buckthorn)........................... dome
Hydrangea..................................... dome
Lavateria.. arching
Magnolia .... arching
Perovskia .... arching
Potentilla .... dome
Roses .... arching
Tamarix .... arching
Ulex... dome
Yucca .... spiky dome

FURTHER INFORMATION

FURTHER READING

Billington, Jill *New Classic Gardens* (Rockport Publishers Inc., 2011)

Brickell,Christopher (ed.) *RHS A–Z Encyclopaedia of Garden Plants* (Dorling Kindersley Ltd, 2003)

Brickell, Christopher, and Joyce, David *RHS Pruning and Training* (Dorling Kindersley, 2006)

Christopher, Marina, et al *Late Summer Flowers* (Frances Lincoln Publishers Ltd, 2011)

Collins Aura Garden Handbooks (Harper Collins Publishers and Aura Editions)

Cubey, Janet, and Merrick, Judith *RHS Plant Finder 2011–2012* (Royal Horticultural Society, 2011) ISBN 978-1-4053-4176-9

Greenwood, Pippa, and Halstead, Andrew *RHS Pests and Diseases* (Dorling Kindersley Ltd, 2009)

Hessayon, Dr D.G. *The Expert Series* (PBI Publications)

Keble, Martin W. *Concise British Flora in Colour* (Sphere Books, 1979)

Philips, Roger, and Rix, Martyn *The Pan Garden Plants Series* (Pan Books Ltd)

Pope, Nori, and Sandra *Colour by Design – planting the contemporary garden* (Conran Octopus Ltd, 1998)

Wilson, Andrew *The Book of Plans for Small Gardens* (Mitchell Beazley, 2007)

USEFUL WEBSITES

www.pamelajohnson.co.uk
Pamela Johnson Garden Design.

www.andersonlandscapedesign.co.uk
Anderson Landscape and Garden Design.

www.rhs.org.uk
The Royal Horticultural Society – Gardening advice and information.

www.rhs.org.uk/shows-events
The Royal Horticultural Society flower shows and events.

www.communities.gov.uk/publications/planning andbuilding/pavingfrontgardens
Government information about legislation regarding paving of front gardens.

www.wrap.org.uk
Waste and Resources Action Programme (information about recycling and sourcing compost).

www.recyclenow.com

www.metoffice.gov.uk
Weather and climate information.

www.nhm.ac.uk/nature-online/index.html
Native plants by postcode in the UK.

www.rspb.org
Information about attracting birds into the garden.

www.environment-agency.gov.uk/business/
sectors/91970.aspx
Green roof information.

www.nccpg.com
Garden plant conservation charity.

www.ngs.org.uk
Gardens open for charity.

www.planthuntersfair.co.uk
www.rareplantfair.co.uk
Specialist plant fairs.

www.southportflowershow.org.uk
Southport flower show.

www.flowershow.org.uk
Harrogate flower show.

www.nationaltrust.org.uk
Contains details of properties owned by the National
Trust and their gardens.

www.johninnes.info
John Innes loam-based compost.

GARDENS TO VISIT IN THE UK

England

Cheshire
Ness Botanic Gardens, Ness, Neston, South Wirral
CH64 4AY

Devon
Burrow Farm Gardens, Dalwood, Axminster, East
Devon EX13 7ET

Stone Lane Gardens, Stone Farm, Chagford, Devon
TQ13 8JU

RHS Garden Rosemoor, Great Torrington, Devon
EX38 8PH

East Sussex
Great Dixter, High Park Close, Northiam, Rye,
East Sussex TN31 6PH

Essex
RHS Garden Hyde Hall, Westerns Approach,
Rettendon, Chelmsford, Essex CM3 8AT

Beth Chatto Gardens, Elmstead Market, Colchester,
Essex CO7 7DB

Gloucestershire
Hidcote Manor Gardens, Hidcote, Bartrim,
Gloucestershire GL55 6LR

Hampshire
Mottisfont Abbey Garden (National Trust), Romsey,
Hampshire SO51 0LP

Hinton Ampner (National Trust), Bramdean,
Near Alresford, Hampshire SO2 4OL

Gilbert White's House, Selbourne, Hampshire
GU34 3JH

Herefordshire
Bryan's Ground, Stapleton (Near Presteigne),
Herefordshire LD8 2LP

Hampton Court Castle Garden, Hope-Under-
Dinmore, Leominster, Herefordshire HR6 0PN

Stockton Bury Gardens, Kimbolton, Nr. Leominster,
Herefordshire HR6 0HB

Kent
Sissinghurst Castle (National Trust), Biddenden
Road, Near Cranbrook, Kent TN17 2AB

London
Chelsea Physic Garden, 66 Royal Hospital Road,
London SW3 4HS

Kensington Roof Garden, 99 High Street,
Kensington, London W8 5SA

Royal Botanical Gardens Kew, 18 Station Parade,
Kew, London TW9 3PZ

Northamptonshire
Cottesbrooke Hall, Northampton NN6 8PF

Coton Manor Garden, Coton, Northampton
NN6 8RQ

Northumberland
The Alnwick Garden, Denwick Lane, Alnwick,
Northumberland NE66 1YU

Oxfordshire
Brook Cottage, Well Lane, Alkerton, Nr Banbury,
Oxfordshire OX15 6NL

Pettifers
Lower Wardington, Banbury OX17 1RY

Shropshire
The Dorothy Clive Garden, Willoughbridge,
Market Drayton, Shropshire TF9 4EU

Wollerton Old Hall, Wollerton, Market Drayton,
Shropshire TF9 3NA

Somerset
Forde Abbey, Chard, Somerset TA20 4LU

Lower Severalls, Crewkerne, Somerset TA18 7NX

East Lambrook Manor, East Lambrook,
South Petherton TA13 5HH

Surrey
Hannah Peschar Sculpture Garden, Black and White
Cottage, Standon Lane, Ockley, Surrey RH5 5QR

RHS Garden Wisley, Woking, GU23 6QB

Loseley House and Garden, Guildford, Surrey
GU3 1HS

West Sussex
Denmans Gardens, Denmans Lane, Fontwell,
Arundel, West Sussex BN18 0SU

Cass Sculpture Foundation, Goodwood, Chichester,
West Sussex PO18 0QP

Wakehurst Place (Kew), Selsfield Rd, Ardingly,
West Sussex RH17 6TN

Yorkshire
RHS Garden Harlow Carr, Crag Lane, Harrogate
HG3 1QB

Wales

Bodnant Gardens, Bodnant Road, Tal-Y-Cafn, Conwy
LL28 5RE

Glansevern Hall, Revel, Berriew, Welshpool, Powys
SY21 8AH

Veddw House Garden, Devauden, Monmouthshire,
NP16 6PH

Scotland

Crarae Garden, Minard, Inveraray, Argyll PA32 8YA

Achamore Gardens, Isle of Gigha Heritage Trust,
Craft Workshops, Isle of Gigha, Argyll PA41 7AA

Benmore Botanic Garden, Dunoon, Argyll PA23 8QU

GLOSSARY

acid loving a plant which cannot tolerate alkaline soil

annual a plant that grows, flowers and sets seed in one year

aspect the geographical direction that a garden faces

biennial a plant that grows one year, and flowers and sets seed in the next year

bare legs bare stems on the lower parts of a plant

bare rooted plants plants which have been dug out of the ground and sold without a pot

bract modified leaf, usually looking different to a leaf and more like a petal

dry shade refers to ground which is both dry and shaded from light

leggy describes a plant with long, unsightly lower stems

adapted to refers to plants or animals which have genetically changed in order to survive a specific environment

base rock the layer of rock beneath subsoil

conditions the growing environment including type of soil, water, light, food and air

compost plant material which has been rotted down together, used for potting or to improve soil

cultivated plants plants which have been bred from wild plants

deciduous describes plants that drop their leaves in winter

depth of field the distance between the nearest and furthest objects

dormant refers to a period of time when active growth of a plant has stopped

ericaceous without lime; ericaceous compost has no lime in it and is suitable for acid loving plants

evergreen describes plants that keep their leaves in winter

exposed site place with no shelter from the weather

fastigiate refers to a tree with upright erect branches

focal point a feature that the eye is drawn to; a strong structural element such as a key plant or sculpture

foliage leaves

free-draining refers to ground which water will easily drain through

frosted damaged by frost

hardy able to survive frost and cold

half hardy needs protection against cold in winter

heeled-in temporarily planted in soil

frost tender not able to survive very low temperatures

herbaceous perennial soft-stemmed perennial which dies back in winter and sends out new growth the following spring

growing season   time of year in which plants grow, usually from spring to autumn

humus   rotted plant material which is no longer able to decompose

mulch   layer put on top of the soil, to protect plants and nourish the soil

microclimate   unique environment, often created by the warmth generated by buildings in cities

National Collection   specially preserved collection of every known cultivar of a particular plant species, such as *Euphorbia*

native conditions   environment in which a plant originally grew and flourished

new wood   a shrub's stems which are less than two years old

neutral soil   having neutral pH, neither acid nor alkaline

nutrients   food, minerals and salts required by plants

officinalis   common species name used for a plant with herbal and possibly medicinal properties

old wood   a shrub's stems which are more than two years old

organic   refers to natural plant material and the absence of manmade contaminants

organic matter   a composition of natural plant materials

perennial   soft-stemmed plant which lives for more than three years

root ball   mass of roots formed by a plant

plant colonies   groups of plants growing together in the same environment

root bound   refers to a plant that has outgrown its container, with the roots growing through the bottom

self seeded   refers to a plant growing from seed which was distributed naturally by the parent plant

site analysis   study of a garden or place

staking   supporting

subsoil   layer of soil beneath topsoil

sustainable   creating little waste, re-using and recycling as much as possible

topsoil   top layer of soil in a garden

tree canopy   covering of leaves on a tree

under-planting   low plants growing under the canopy of larger ones

variegated   refers to leaves with areas having no green chlorophyll, caused by a natural mutation

water table   the naturally occurring body of underground water

ACKNOWLEDGEMENTS

PHOTOGRAPHY

Cover

Front cover photography by Clive Nichols; back cover photography by Pamela Johnson.

Text

Photographs taken by Jill Anderson: page 9 Chelsea garden by Ulf Njordfell; page 10 Chelsea Flower Show garden by Andy Sturgeon; page 11 Chelsea Flower Show garden by Tom Stuart-Smith; page 12 Foxhills garden; page 13 Chelsea Flower Show; page 14 RHS Wisley; page 15; page 17 Loseley Garden; page 18; page 21 private garden; page 22 Chelsea Flower Show garden by Andy Sturgeon; page 23 private garden; page 24 Hampton Court Flower Show garden designed by Jill Anderson; page 26 Chelsea Flower Show garden by Adam Frost; page 27 private garden; page 28 Loseley Garden; page 29 Loseley Garden; page 33; page 43 Chelsea Flower Show Garden designed by Mark Gregory; page 44 Hampton Court Flower Show; page 45 Loseley Garden; page 46 Chelsea Flower Show garden by Ulf Njordfell; page 47 Gilbert White Garden; page 48; page 49; page 50 Chelsea Flower Show by Mark Gregory; page 51; page 52 Chelsea Flower Show garden by Adam Frost; page 53 Chelsea Flower Show garden by Mark Gregory; page 54 Hampton Court Flower Show; page 55; page 56; page 57 Chelsea Flower Show by Andy Sturgeon; page 73 Chelsea Flower Show garden by Luciano Guibbilei; page 74; page 75; page 77 Chelsea Flower Show; page 78 Loseley Garden; page 80; page 81 Loseley Garden; page 83 Chelsea Flower Show; page 119; page 120; page 121 Hampton Court Flower Show; page 123; page 127; page 128; page 131 Chelsea Flower Show.

Photographs taken by Pamela Johnson: frontispiece; page 30 Southern France; page 31 private garden; page 32 Barcelona, Spain and Southern France; page 33; page 35; page 38 *Papaver* 'Patty's Plum; page 39 private garden; page 40 private garden; page 58; page 60 Picos de Europa, Northern Spain; page 62; pages 64–67; page 68; page 69; page 76 private garden; pages 85–88; page 91 Neil's Garden Centre, Wandsworth, London; page 93; page 94; page 103; page 105 RHS Garden at Wisley; page 106 Burrow Farm Nursery, Devon; page 107 Burrow Farm Garden, Devon; page 109 Neil's Garden Centre, Wandsworth, London; page 110 Chelsea Flower Show; page 111; page 112 Burrow Farm Garden, Devon; pages 113–115; page 116 Architectural Plants, Surrey; page 122 Great Dixter Garden, East Sussex; page 124; page 130 Neil's Garden Centre, Wandsworth, London; page 132 RHS Garden Wisley, Surrey; page 133 Great Dixter Garden, East Sussex; page 134; page 136; page 138 Trevarrick House Somerset; page 139; pages 141–143, page 144 Great Dixter Garden, East Sussex, page 146.

Photographs taken by Clive Nichol: page 8; page 16; page 42 Veddw Garden; page 72 Pashley Manor Garden; page 84; page 118; page 147.

Many thanks to the following for allowing their gardens to be photographed: Gabrielle and Michael Bray; Gilbert White's House; Loseley House Guildford; Royal Horticultural Society; Mike and Ali Welton; Kim and Duncan Varley; Trevarrick House, Somerset; Mr & Mrs Hibbert, Gloucestershire; Burrows Farm Garden, Devon; Neil's Garden Centre, Wandsworth, London; Architectural Plants, Surrey; Great Dixter Garden, East Sussex; RHS Garden Wisley, Surrey

Thanks to the following for help with proof-reading: Carol Swaisland, Cath Pettyfer, Clive Stone, Colin Campbell, Gethyn Davies and Kath Wurcbacher.

INDEX